Fly to Honor

FLY TO HONOR

NEIL DUFFY

Published by Duffy Publishing

The author wishes to acknowledge and thank the following publishers and individuals for permission to quote them or their work: Delmor Jacobs and Jim Clader, *Lacrosse: The Ancient Game;* Tim O'Brien, *The Things They Carried,* Houghton Mifflin Harcourt; Lester I. Tenney, *My Hitch in Hell* ©Potomac Books/An Imprint of the University of Nebraska Press; Viktor E. Frankel "Man's Search for Meaning" by Viktor E. Frankl, Copyright © 1959, 1962, 1984, 1992 by Viktor E. Frankl, Reprinted by permission of Beacon Press, Boston; Joe Erhmann *InSideOut Coaching, How Sports can Transform Lives;* Daniel Pink, *A Whole New Mind;* Gus Heningburg for Bob Bianchi; Mr. Conrad M. Hall; the family of Mr. Guy Friddell; the Tunstall family for W. Brooke Tunstall; Coach Mark Johnson (and for his late father, Bob Johnson); and several unnamed naval officers. The author has attempted to secure permissions from the following individuals and publishers: General Colin Powell, *It Worked for Me;* Steven Pressfield, *The Virtues of War;* Stanley Tyron *Prisoners of Hope;* the Towson HS Alumni Newsletter; Paulo Coelho, *The Witch of Portobello;* Neil deGrasse Tyson. The author offers apologies for any use not authorized explicitly and will rectify the issue in subsequent editions, pending notification. It is hoped that the author has appropriately applied the standard of "fair use" in some cases (Einstein, Rousseau, Emerson, LT (SEAL) Looney).

Cover art and design by Mike Gottleib
Layout by Jonathan Gullery of Budget Book Design
Printed by Ron Pramschufer of RJ Communications and BooksJustBooks.com

ISBN: 978-0-9753686-6-4

CONTENTS

THANK YOU FOR
YOUR KIND WORDS!

"*Fly to Honor*, through Jack Turnbull (and so many others), provides us a 'today's' historic and cultural glimpse of what it meant and what it took to play the Creator's game. The values demonstrated by warriors of the past are as much needed today as they were in the past. Honor and Respect will always be the warrior way as the Creator's game mandates."

Sid Jamieson
Bucknell University
Former Men's Lacrosse Coach, Bucknell University
(1968-2005)
"Spirit of Tewaaraton" Award 2005
USILA "Howdy Myers Man of the Year" 1986, 1996
USILA "Frenchy Julien Service Award" 2005

"A must-read for all lacrosse fans…a profound and captivating tribute to one of the game's most memorable figures."

Dom Starsia
Head Men's Lacrosse Coach, University of Virginia
1999, 2003, 2006, 2011 NCAA Division I National Champions
National Lacrosse Hall of Fame
USILA "Howdy Myers Man of the Year" 2006

"Neil Duffy represents the very best about our sport, The Creator's Game. *Fly to Honor* is important and inspiring. You'll read it more than once."

Mike Hanna
Director of Athletics
Hobart College
USILA "Frenchy Julien Service Award" 1986

"*Fly to Honor* offers an ageless and timeless gift of core values that will serve a young man or woman throughout their lives. As a collegiate coach of nearly forty years, this both brings back the 'magical' of feeling my first, hand-carved lacrosse stick, and now offers a refreshing renewal of values for team leadership. This is must-read for leadership that could not have come at a better time in the history of our sport."

Ray Rostan
Head Lacrosse Coach, Hampden-Sydney College
Assistant Coach, Team USA 2002

"*Fly to Honor* is a must-read for players, parents, and coaches of all levels. The lessons and messages that Robbie continues to learn from Red Hawk are applicable today. As caretakers of the Creator's Game, we are all responsible to play, cheer, and coach this game with great honor. The game of lacrosse has a bright future, but for it to shine its brightest, we must embrace its glorious past."

Mike Murphy
Head Men's Lacrosse Coach, Colgate University
Former assistant coach, United States
Military Academy at West Point

"Hopefully, all aspiring lacrosse players will read Coach Duffy's novels *The Spirit in the Stick* and *Fly to Honor*. I have asked all of our players to read *Spirit* and plan to do the same with *Fly to Honor*. Both novels use the game as an avenue to teach valuable life lessons while providing the reader with tremendous insight into the history of our great game."

J.P. Stewart
Head Men's Lacrosse Coach,
Virginia Wesleyan College

"*Fly to Honor* is an amazing history lesson of our great sport that captures the imagination and describes all that is great about lacrosse."

Steve Koudelka
Head Lacrosse Coach, Lynchburg College

"I was thrilled to hear that Neil Duffy was releasing *Fly to Honor*. I was eager to return to the lessons of character, leadership, and service that Neil was able to convey in *The Spirit in the Stick* in such an entertaining yet impactful manner. For those of us who have experienced the game of lacrosse, have respected its roots in Native American culture and history, and have admired the contributions of men like Lt. Col. Jack Turnbull to the game of lacrosse and our country, *Fly to Honor* is an inspiration.

Erin Quinn
Director of Athletics, Middlebury College

For

Richie Meade and the USA Men's Lacrosse Team

In Honor of and as a "Thank You" to

Admiral Charles R. Larson, USNA '58
Bob Reifsnyder, USNA '59
Captain Jim Lewis, USNA '66
LTC & Mrs. Mike Sheedy, USMC (Ret.)
Navy Lacrosse–Past, Present, Future
The United States Naval Academy
"S.F."

and in Memory of
my late father, George A. Duffy
(one of the Greatest Navy Lacrosse Fans in History!)
M.G. Buchanan
(*the* Greatest Navy Lacrosse Fan in History!)
LT (SEAL) Brendan Looney, USNA '04
Bob Sandell
W. Brooke Tunstall
Sue Cassidy
Lorraine Donder

INTRODUCTION

As current and former head lacrosse coaches at the United States Military Academy, we have had the honor and privilege of working with hundreds of truly special and dedicated young men preparing to become officers in our country's military. We watched those young men go from (sometimes) shaggy-haired civilians, through the Induction process and Plebe Year, and grow with each passing semester into commissioned officers.

We then watched these young men assume positions of immediate leadership, responsibility, and accountability and answer the call of duty in every corner of the globe and in just about every conceivable way—again and again.

We have seen our players get promoted, receive military decorations, visited them in hospitals after being wounded in combat, attended their weddings, change-of-command ceremonies, retirements, and, yes, funerals.

Two of us also enjoyed the honor of serving as coaches of the United States Men's Lacrosse team, where we were privileged to work with our country's finest players—all driven to represent their country with pride and respect and to their fullest capabilities.

As we feel a special kinship with Jack Turnbull of Johns Hopkins University and his collegiate, club, and international (Jack was a member of the last lacrosse team to represent the United States in an Olympic Games—Los Angeles in 1932) playing career, as well as his exemplary and heroic service to our country, we could not be more eager or proud to commend to you *Fly to Honor*. We also could not be more personally or professionally supportive of and warmed by the dedications that the author offers to Coach Meade, CAPT Lewis, ADM Larson, LT (SEAL) Looney and others.

In *Fly to Honor*, the story of Robbie Jones and his relationship with his special lacrosse stick and its original steward, the Native American boy Red Hawk, begun in *The Spirit in the Stick*, continues as the incredible story of Jack Turnbull comes to life.

Those who knew Jack or watched him play will tell you that he was the greatest they had seen. Beyond his national- and Olympic-championship and First-Team All-American level of play on the field and his well-respected and gentlemanly behavior off the field, it is his truly inspiring service to his country by which he is most remembered. His ultimate sacrifice in 1944 is commemorated even today in the form of the Lt. Col. John I. Turnbull Award, presented annually to the outstanding attackman in each of the three college divisions, and the Turnbull-Reynolds Trophy (Pete Reynolds was another JHU lacrosse player who lost his life in World War II–of whom you will learn more later in the book), awarded to a Johns Hopkins University lacrosse player to recognize sportsmanship and leadership.

Lacrosse's ancient history is rooted in the Native American warrior ethos. It is not a coincidence, we think, that four major lacrosse awards (before the relatively recent establishment of the Tewaaraton Trophy–the "Heisman Trophy of Lacrosse") are named for players who became military officers and died in the service of our country. The award for Outstanding Defenseman is named in honor of "Father" Bill Schmeisser of Johns Hopkins, who, though not a military officer is credited with being the inspiration behind the placement of memorial flags on the nets at Johns Hopkins (of which you will learn more later in this book). The (Navy) Lieutenant (junior grade) Donald MacLaughlin, Jr. Award is named for a former Navy Lacrosse player and team captain, Class of 1963, whose plane went down on a combat mission in South Vietnam in 1966 and is presented to the nation's top midfielder. The Outstanding Goaltender award is named in memory of Ensign C. Markland Kelly, who grew up in Baltimore and played at the University of Maryland. Kelly took off from the USS *Hornet* on an escort mission in support of the Battle of Midway on June 4, 1942 and was reported missing in action. The country's top player is recognized in memory of our own 1967 West Point graduate, First Lieutenant Raymond Enners, who perished in ground action in Vietnam in 1968. And Jack's Award, of course.

As with this book's predecessor, you will learn about the lives of great people–particularly Jack–and lessons of character, courage, generosity, gratitude, and sacrifice that we think will stay with you.

You will also be treated to a rich collection of letters from scores of Turnbull Award recipients–some of the greatest players the game has known–in the special "Legacy" section at the end.

As you enjoy reading *Fly to Honor*, we would ask you to be actively mindful of the service and sacrifice of the selfless and courageous men and women who have worn–and continue to wear–our country's uniform.

United States Military Academy Lacrosse Coaches

Jim Adams (1958-1969)
Peg Pisano for Al Pisano (1970-1976)
Dick Edell (1977-1983)
Jack Emmer (1984-2005)
Joe Alberici (2006–present)
July 2014

PREFACE

W HEN I began to write *The Spirit in the Stick* in 1999, I could never have imagined the impact it would have on my life. The research and writing of the story was its own reward. But once the manuscript and final copy made their way into the hands of readers, I suddenly, and completely unexpectedly, began to hear from people all over the country—and world—about what the Game of Lacrosse had meant to them. The gratitude that overtook me was immediate and overwhelming. You see, the project was not originally intended to be published and would never have happened at all if not for the good grace of people like Coach Bob Scott, CAPT Jim Lewis, USNA '66, MAJ R. Bruce Turnbull, USMA '57, Dr. Tom Vennum, and scores of others. Even from its earliest beginnings, I never considered the story or the project my own but rather the collective sum of the goodness that those good people, and the Game itself, shared with me.

The Spirit in the Stick connected me with thousands of people I would not have met otherwise and enriched my life in ways that I never knew existed. The inspiration and support of those people has kept this project alive and active on a daily basis. I have known all along that there was a sequel to be written—actually there are several more stories to tell to complete the story of this amazing stick. *Fly to Honor* is a story that needed to be written about Jack Turnbull and so many others who have surrendered their lives in the service of our country.

The timing of the debut of *Fly to Honor* could not have been more personally meaningful. I offer the initial printing for Richie Meade–my coach, friend, mentor, and, more importantly, my daughter's godfather–and his USA Lacrosse Team as they compete in the 2014 Federation of International Lacrosse (FIL) World Championships in Denver (and as a gift to all of the teams). I also offer it in honor of the Tewaaraton Foundation's 2014 Award recipients CAPT Jim Lewis, USNA '66, the *Tewaaraton Legends* Award, and the late LT (SEAL) Brendan Looney, USNA '04, the *Spirit of Tewaaraton* Award.

I also have just arrived at the thirty year anniversary of my graduation from the United States Naval Academy (where has the time gone?), and would like to express my deep gratitude to that institution, the Navy Lacrosse program–with which I have been fortunate to maintain contact with all these years–as well as my classmates, teammates, and companymates. I must specifically thank ADM Charles Larson '58 for his gracious support and impact in my life, my high school football coach, Bob Reifsnyder '59, and my sponsors at USNA, LTC Mike Sheedy, USMC (Ret.), his wife Cathy and their girls, Lisa, Jennifer, and Erin. I could not be more fortunate or grateful to be connected to such a great program, school, and people. April 2014 is also the ten year anniversary of the first printing of *The Spirit in the Stick*–so it seemed a nice time to follow up on that story.

I also need to convey my deepest gratitude to the scores of Turnbull Award recipients whose generosity of spirit has enriched this process in ways that have dwarfed all of the goodness that had come in previously, taking the depth and strength of this project to an entirely new level.

Though I'll never be able to properly thank them all, I hope *Fly to Honor* will serve as a modest and collective "Thank You" to all of the people mentioned here, the United States Naval Academy, and to the Game, itself.

As with *The Spirit in the Stick*, this story has largely written itself, buoyed by the good grace and generosity of scores of people. Please consider this to be a work of "historical fiction/fantasy" in which I have endeavored to remain true to the factual history–and, perhaps more importantly, spirit–of all characters, particularly Jack Turnbull and his family–especially his father and brother, Douglas C. Turnbull, Senior and Junior. Captain Lewis and Jack's family, most notably his nephews (and Doug's sons) Bruce and Jack, and grand-niece, Susan Turnbull Generazio, have, as in my last story, allowed appropriate and spirit-based "writer's license" to connect the main themes of the story. Once again, perhaps it is best left to the reader to decipher fact from fiction.

"Respect the Game!"

N.V.D.
Virginia Beach, VA
10 JUL 2014

PROLOGUE

"I want my children and my grandchildren to know that war is horrible."

Lester L. Tenney
My Hitch in Hell

Convent Gesticht van Den H. Joseph
Petegem-aan-de-Leie/Deinze, Belgium, 18 OCT 1944

"Colonel Turnbull? Colonel Turnbull?"

"Colonel Turnbull? Can you hear me?" Sister Christine whispered into Jack's ear in her best English as she gently held his shoulders.

"Please sip this water."

Sister Lutgarde held Jack's hand and desperately prayed for his survival.

LIEUTENANT Colonel John Iglehart "Jack" Turnbull, United States Army Air Corps, lay motionless and unresponsive on a cot in a convent located about nine miles southwest of Ghent, Belgium clinging to a barely detectable pulse and breath. The nuns had helped rescue Jack from the wreckage of one of the two United States B-24 bombers that had crashed nearby and about a mile apart earlier that afternoon.

Jack was the only survivor of the crashes–though the two waist gunners in his plane were miraculously able to parachute from the aircraft as it plummeted to the ground following what was probably a midair collision between them in a thunderstorm-filled sky. Those two airmen suffered minor injuries and were quickly moved from the site to receive medical care.

A cursory scan of the scene by first responders reported no other survivors. A Canadian unit in the area began the grim task of recovering bodies from the wreckage for proper disposition. After removing twelve victims and arriving finally upon Jack, one of their officers was shocked to detect a faint pulse.

"I have a survivor! I have a survivor!" the officer yelled to his comrades.

Help came in the form of several soldiers and three nuns from the nearby convent. Knowing that Medevac assistance had left earlier, the nuns volunteered to aid Jack until help could return. The crew extracted Jack gingerly from the wreckage of his aircraft and transported him on a stretcher provided by the nuns to the relative comfort of their modest convent infirmary.

Jack remained unconscious, opening his eyes perhaps a dozen times and only briefly during the night at the convent while the nuns sat vigil.

The women whispered frequently to the American aviator, "Colonel Turnbull? Colonel Turnbull, please stay with us. We are trying to get you help."

A local doctor arrived at sunrise the next morning but pronounced Jack close to death. "He is certainly suffering from massive internal injuries. We cannot risk moving him. I am afraid there is little we can do."

During the day, the nuns were able to nurse Jack to a state of quasi-consciousness—but only for the briefest of periods.

When Jack was able to move or attempt speech, he groaned in the faintest whisper, and mostly-unintelligible words that may have been, "Mellish," and "flag."

The nuns continued their vigil. The sisters rotated duties from holding Jack's hand to whispering and listening to him, then dabbing his lips with water; but constantly praying. They could do little else.

Of the few words the nuns were able to decipher was "flag," which Jack seemed to whisper several times while feebly motioning his right hand toward his heart.

The sisters were not sure of what Jack was attempting to communicate, but he seemed to be gesturing to the zipped compartment in his flight suit immediately below his heart and nametag. The nuns unzipped the compartment and removed a small–perhaps eighteen by twenty four inch–United States flag rolled and secured by three thin ribbons–one white, one red, one blue.

Jack desperately strained in a whisper, "O…pen…"

Sister Seraphine untied the ribbons, unfurled the flag, and discovered two sheets of paper. Jack offered a barely-perceptible nod and again strained a whisper, "y…es."

The nun began to read silently the first sheet of paper. She numbly passed it to her cohorts and then did the same with the next. The three sisters stared at each other in disbelief but said nothing.

"Send," Jack whispered still without opening his eyes. "Mellish."

"There," the nuns were certain Jack was breathing his last words, "are," Sister Christine leaned her ear to Jack's lips, "more." "Please…" A minute later, "…find."

Jack became unconscious again.

Then several minutes later, he whispered again, "Please…" Yet another interminable delay, "…send…. Thank… you."

"Colonel Turnbull," the nuns begged.

"Colonel Turnbull? …Please…."

That's what stories are for. Stories are for joining the past to the future. Stories are for those late hours in the night when you can't remember how you got from where you were to where you are. Stories are for eternity, when memory is erased, when there is nothing to remember except the story.

Tim O'Brien
The Things They Carried

ROBBIE'S JOURNEY CONTINUES

For hours I stood hacking at the icy ground. The guard passed by, insulting me, and once again, I communicated with my beloved. More and more I felt that she was present, that she was with me: I had the feeling that I was able to touch her, able to stretch out my hand and grasp hers. The feeling was very strong: she was there. Then, at that very moment, a bird flew down silently and perched just in front of me, on the heap of soil which I had dug up from the ditch, and looked steadily at me.

Viktor E. Frankel
Man's Search for Meaning

EVERYTHING was brighter, sharper, deeper, richer–better–now for Robbie. He could see and *feel* more colors and hear more sounds. His sensitivity to, and appreciation for, the beauty and majesty of nature–all living things, the Earth, the cosmos–rocketed to new heights the instant his eyes stared into the red hawk's eyes a month earlier. His understanding of the essence of the human condition had leapt tenfold in the last year. History was no longer a collection of dry, dull, dusty, inert names, dates, and arcane facts–but stories of *real* people experiencing *real* emotions, *real* challenges, *real* events, and living *real* lives.

His knowledge and understanding of the past and vision for the future had also become more keenly honed, but, much more importantly, he had also learned that neither of those mattered nearly as much as the present—the *now*. His fourteen-year-old way of thinking and acting was now long gone.

Robbie's magical lacrosse stick had brought him more insight and taught him more in the preceding year than he could have ever imagined, and his relationship with Captain Lewis and Red Hawk had changed his life forever. He was eager to learn more and knew he was still only scratching the surface of this amazing story. The lives of the men who had the stick before him—the previous stewards—were all models of leadership, service, sacrifice, and gratitude. The meanings of the carvings on his stick were rich and compelling stories of their own.

What would come next? He wondered.

Robbie reminded himself of what the young Native American boy Red Hawk, who had befriended him in his dreams through the spirit in the stick, had shared with him on his last visit. "I believe this is a stick of life. It is a stick of honor. It is a stick of respect. Above all, though, I think the true spirit of this stick is one of hope," Red Hawk had shared.

What would he ask Captain Lewis? What would he ask Red Hawk? Whom else would he meet? Where else would he go?

Robbie stood by himself in the exact location where he had met Captain Lewis for the first time nearly one year earlier and waited for him to arrive. He held his special stick softly in his hands and had its leather bag slung over his right shoulder. They were there to celebrate the one-year anniversary of their meeting. A full moon was beginning to rise—like during his first meeting with Captain Lewis. This time, though, Robbie was fully aware of the moon and its significance, having actually grown accustomed to feeling Red Hawk's presence on days like these. The boy was already beginning to formulate his questions for tonight.

Lewis had told Robbie that he would be bringing some guests and, as usual, arrived exactly on time. "Hi, Robbie. Great to see you." Lewis greeted Robbie warmly with a handshake.

"Let me introduce you to Major Bruce Turnbull and his wife Jerri."

Robbie immediately registered the name—Turnbull—and his mind raced to determine how the couple might be connected to his special stick and, therefore, him.

Robbie greeted the couple with his usual politeness.

"Robbie, please call me Bruce. It is a pleasure to meet you. Captain Lewis has shared a great deal about his and your relationship with Jerri and me."

"Robbie, Bruce is the son of Doug and the nephew of Jack Turnbull. I know that you learned a great deal about both of those men—but I thought it might be a good time for you to meet Bruce so that you may ask him some questions," Captain Lewis offered.

Like so many other times in the last year, Robbie's heart raced with excitement and his mind began to swirl with thoughts of where he might go and what he might see and learn.

"Robbie, I can't tell you how thrilled I am that you now have that incredible stick that my father and Uncle Jack shared so many years ago," Bruce began as his eyes gazed at Robbie's ancient stick. "They took great care of it and I know that Captain Lewis has done the same for these fifty-some years. You can probably imagine what an honor it was for my father and uncle to be a part of the history of that stick. It has meant so, so much to our family. Jim and I arranged to meet with you today because this is the exact date one hundred years ago when my father received the stick from General Chamberlain! My father was a boy of eleven at that point.

"I always knew of the stick and how important it was to my father, of course, but I did not know of its remarkable magical powers until after my father passed it to Captain Lewis. I remember that after his mother died in 1957, my father carved that beautiful depiction of the Anne Frank book *Het Achterhuis* on the shaft to add to the others. I had recently graduated from West Point at that time. He began to think that he should pass it along to someone else. I haven't seen it since then."

Robbie offered the stick to Bruce. "Would you like to look at it, sir?"

"Thank you, Robbie, I would love to!"

Bruce's body warmed as he touched the stick. He felt his father's and uncle's presence immediately as he held this piece of history. He blinked back tears.

"My goodness, Robbie, there are the carvings my father and Jack did when they had it," Bruce marveled. Jerri stood by in awe as she had never seen the stick—but had only heard of it.

Bruce spoke quietly to the boy as his thumb caressed each carving, "So you have learned of all of these carvings? Running Water's, Red Hawk's, Lieutenant Casey's, General Chamberlain's, Jack's, my father's, … and this one must be Jim's?"

Robbie nodded with Bruce's pauses at each notch on the stick. "Yes, sir."

"Jim," Bruce turned to Lewis, "I hope you'll share with me the meaning of your carving at some point. I am sure that it has tremendous significance to you."

"It does. I would be glad to," Lewis replied eagerly.

"And the writing, Robbie?" Bruce continued as he turned the stick on its edge.

"Yes, sir, that, too," the boy replied proudly.

"Jim, it seems that you and Red Hawk have done a great job in sharing the history of the stick with Robbie," Bruce concluded.

"I've tried, sir. I think Red Hawk has done most of it, though."

Bruce continued to hold the stick and stare at it with great reverence as he maneuvered it through every possible angle. "You know, Robbie, my father kept a detailed journal of his relationship with the stick and Red Hawk. When I first read it, I was completely spellbound. My father was meticulous in everything he did. He was also extremely religious and for a long time seemed to have a very difficult time believing that the 'visits' from Red Hawk were actually real. He did not share any of it with his parents and only let me see his writings after he had passed the stick to Jim. And, of course, the stick had an incredible role in the life of my Uncle Jack, as well.

"I have been fortunate to get some idea of what this stick has meant to its stewards through my father's and Jack's writings, but I know that you must have a much greater appreciation for what it means because you have *experienced* its power firsthand. I know that you have already learned and grown a great deal, Robbie. Jerri and I hope that we may add to your experience with the stick. We'll do our best to help you. Captain Lewis, of course, will continue to be a part of your learning, as well."

Lewis, the Turnbulls, and Robbie began to walk slowly along the path where Robbie and Lewis had saved a fledgling bird last year.

"I hope you don't mind that Captain Lewis has gotten Jerri and me pretty much up-to-date on the visits that you have shared with him—so I think we have a sense of some of the scenes you have experienced concerning my father and Uncle Jack. Is there anything I can help you with now, Robbie?" Bruce offered.

"No, I don't mind at all—that's great. I have been trying to write down the stories that I have learned from Captain Lewis and Red Hawk—just like I think your father did," Robbie responded.

"There is so much more I would like to know about them, though. Red Hawk has taken me to some amazing places to see them—and so many others, too. I still don't really even know what is possible. Do you think I might be able to see your father's journals at some point?"

Bruce smiled. "That would be easy, Robbie. I have more stuff than you can imagine. My father and uncle would be thrilled for you to see it all. We can decide how to share that part as we go along. Jim has told me that he shared the letter my father wrote him on his high school graduation and a couple of other pieces. The entire collection is in the thousands of pages—I'm not sure exactly how many—probably two or three thousand from my father alone. Jack's papers are in the hundreds. Not only did my father keep a diary—but he also kept and filed just about every piece of correspondence that he ever received. He also made carbon copies of what he considered to be his most important outbound hand-written letters, as well–including all of the ones he sent to Jim." Bruce looked over at Lewis who gave him a smile admitting that his records were probably not as well kept as Doug's.

"My father lived to be ninety-two years old and passed on in 1996. When he wasn't busy being 'The World's Happiest Grandfather,' as he used to describe himself, he spent a good deal of time in his last few years organizing his papers. It really is a treasure to our family. I have spent a pretty good amount of time editing the papers with notes and information that might otherwise be lost to history. My father willed that the collection remain in our family–so I am in possession of it all now. He said he initially thought to pass it along to Jim–but realized that he could accomplish more if he gave it to us to enjoy and allow Jim the actual relationship with Red Hawk and the other stewards. I think he was probably right. I think Jim would agree that he has not been deprived of a single thing in this regard and that he has formed his own relationship with Red Hawk and the stick."

Lewis nodded enthusiastically, "I totally agree, Robbie. This is the best way for you to move forward with the stick."

"General Chamberlain's daughter also communicated with Doug for many years–and we have all of that correspondence, as well," Mrs. Turnbull added.

Bruce continued, "It might be good, Robbie, for you to enjoy most of your relationship directly with Red Hawk. And as Jim has supplemented your experience with his own thoughts and writings, perhaps I can send you some things that might be of interest and use, as well. I'd hate to overwhelm you or make your experience more about Doug and Jack than yourself!"

"I think that would be great. Thanks!" Robbie agreed.

"At some point down the road perhaps we can set up a visit for you and your family to come see us in South Carolina and we'll let you look through it all? Not too far down the road–I am eighty-two years old now!" Bruce smiled.

"I would love that," Robbie beamed.

Lewis took over the discussion, "Well, Robbie, Jerri and Bruce have been a big part of my life–which you probably didn't know–and now I have invited them to be a part of your journey and I am sure they'll be glad to help you in any way they can."

Jerri added, "Robbie, we are so excited. Here is our information–phone numbers, address, and e-mail. Please stay in touch with us."

As the group arrived back to their start point, Robbie's parents were waiting there to pick him up. Lewis introduced Bruce and Jerri to Robbie's parents, Mary and John, and his ten-year-old sister Catherine. Mary and John were infinitely more at ease with this meeting compared to last year, though still rather overwhelmed with what this stick had done for and meant to their son.

As the adults got to know each other a little more, a barely perceptible breeze swept softly across Robbie's face eliciting his now-instinctive and immediate reaction to look to the sky. Robbie noticed a hawk circling above them and alighting on a fencepost some thirty or forty yards away. He quietly excused himself, slipped from the discussion, and approached the bird–exactly as he had on his last trip to this park with Lewis a month earlier. As before, the bird invited Robbie to approach by bobbing its head and the boy picked her up.

Lewis had also felt the breeze–a second or two even before Robbie had–and saw Robbie begin to walk toward the hawk. He brought the chat to a quiet pause and slowly directed his eyes toward Robbie and the bird for all to watch. Robbie's parents had not been there for their son's last meeting with the hawk and the Turnbulls had not heard that part of the story.

Despite knowing how powerful and incredible this stick was, this scene surpassed all other aspects of the story for Robbie's mother as she gasped, covered her mouth with her hand, and blinked back tears as Robbie gently lifted the hawk and stared into her eyes in silent communication. The bird cocked her head and softly flapped her wings a few times. Robbie nodded. The bird nodded. Robbie then gracefully lifted the bird back into the sky and slowly walked back to his group.

Robbie smiled at Lewis as he arrived back, "This time *I thanked her.*"

THE BARN

"Many young boys [of our people] are given a small wooden lacrosse stick while they are still in the cradle."
Cayuga Faithkeeper Dao Jao Dre
in Lacrosse: The Ancient Game by Jim Calder

ROBBIE drifted into sleep that night knowing that Red Hawk would be visiting him—for now the eleventh straight full moon—and was ready with an entirely new set of questions to ask and places he might want to see based on his meeting with the Turnbulls. More importantly, his second meeting with the hawk had convinced him that the first one was not just a chance one-time event but rather a much deeper connection with Nature and gave him yet another new perspective on his relationship with Red Hawk, Captain Lewis, and the stick.

"Hi, Robbie," Red Hawk began.

"Hi!" Robbie gushed." I met Major and Mrs. Turnbull this afternoon!"

Red Hawk nodded, as he already knew.

"So you have known them all these years," Robbie offered more as a statement than a question.

"I have never been able to communicate with them directly, you know, but I certainly know who they are and their role in the story of our stick. They have done a great job in preserving Jack and Doug's part of the story."

Robbie's heart jumped a little when Red Hawk said 'our' stick. Despite the fact that Robbie had grown quite accustomed to–and comfortable with–Red Hawk, he still none-the-less marveled at his ability to communicate with a boy his age who had live some two-hundred and fifty years earlier!

"I can't believe how much I have learned from you and everyone else already, Red Hawk," Robbie began. "And now knowing that the Turnbulls are going to be able to help me…it's pretty amazing!"

"Well, Robbie, remember that all of this is designed to pass along the spirit and goodness that has been a part of stick over the centuries. So just keep learning as much as you can and do your best. Remember that the only requirement of being the steward of the stick is to 'Respect the Game' and pass the stick along when you so choose. I am sure that all of the previous stewards–and others like the Turnbulls–will do their very best to help you."

"I know–but it is pretty overwhelming. I don't really even know which way to go right now. Do you have any ideas?"

"I don't have any specific ideas right now, Robbie. It really is a matter of what you want. I'll let you decide," Red Hawk responded, true to form.

"Well, with the Turnbulls now as part of this–do you think you could help me learn more about Doug and Jack?" Robbie asked.

"I'll be glad to try. Where would you like to start?"

"See, that's where I don't even know. Jack and Doug were both pretty amazing players and people, right? Maybe just some more about them that we haven't visited yet?"

"O.K., well, how 'bout we go back to Baltimore in February, 1914? Do you remember what we saw when that package arrived at the Turnbull home?"

"I do. The part where General Chamberlain had sent the stick to Doug? I remember all of it!"

"That's it. But let's watch a little more this time."

"Great! Let's go!"

Red Hawk began the scene where they had left off a few months earlier. Doug had just received a letter written by the daughter of the famous Civil War General Joshua Chamberlain who had died just days before. Included with the letter was the stick, a leather bag to hold the stick, an ancient rawhide lacrosse ball, and a copy of the book Uncle Tom's Cabin *which was signed by the author, Harriett Beecher Stowe, to Chamberlain. The excitement—and more than a little surprise—in the Turnbull home was palpable.*

After quickly reading the enclosed letter and inscription in the book, Doug began to inspect his gifts. He could tell immediately that there was something special about the stick—it had a magical feel to it. He took the old ball, placed it in the stick, and began to cradle.

"As a precocious four-year-old it didn't take Jack long to want to try the stick himself," Red Hawk said with a smile. As Jack reached for the stick, his older brother handed it to him. Jack became startled by how the stick felt—as if he had been shocked. He was confused by its feeling—which was certainly something he would never have experienced or understood. He immediately stared at the stick. Then he stared inquisitively at Doug. His brother was unable to explain the warm and soft electric sensation the stick created when the boys touched it since he had just experienced for the first time himself and was equally perplexed.

After a few minutes, Doug asked for the stick back and Jack followed him to the barn behind their house. Doug began throwing the new ball with his new stick. He instantly felt the power and precision of the stick as he threw.

After a few minutes of using his new stick, Doug handed it back to Jack. The youngster eagerly took the stick and began throwing at the barn. Jack had spent quite a few hours on the barn with Doug, but he felt completely different with the new stick. Though much smaller than his older brother, Jack was able to sling the ball with complete ease with the special stick compared to the much more labored effort required with his regular stick. Jack knew it was special. He continued to look at Doug with confusion and amazement, which quickly started to turn into sheer joy.

The boys traded turns using the special stick while their parents sat nearby absorbing the scene and wondering how Chamberlain had come to send the stick to Doug, junior.

Red Hawk continued his narration, "So, you see, Robbie, even though the stick was originally intended for Doug, junior–General Chamberlain had not met Jack–Doug was extremely generous in allowing Jack to enjoy it as well. I am not sure all brothers would have been so generous and gracious."

The boys played for a few hours that afternoon, creating their own games and competitions with each other.

"Those brothers spent countless hours on that barn–sometimes together like we just saw and sometimes individually. They would alternate between the new stick and their regular ones. Sometimes their sisters joined them. I am sure that the power and magic of the stick helped inspire them to keep working their skills on their 'wall'–their barn," Red Hawk suggested.

Red Hawk continued, "I was able to visit Doug that night–I thought Jack was far too young–at least at that point. I think I took Doug to the scene you and I saw with Chamberlain and Casey at Little Round Top. But there were probably about five hundred more! I spent a lot of time with Doug. You might remember that Doug had the stick for about forty-five years!

"I was able to visit with Jack, as well. I probably started with him when he was about thirteen or fourteen. They were both great men but very different in many ways. Doug was rather gregarious while Jack was usually quite a bit more reserved. They were great brothers to each other and to their three sisters. I think the age difference, which was about six years, probably helped. Jack worshipped Doug.

"Even though Doug was the first–and then only–four-time First-Team All-American for about fifty years, he was always eager to tell people that Jack was a much better lacrosse player than he was. Jack was a three-time First-Team All-American and almost certainly would have been again but he graduated in three years and chose not to return to Hopkins for a fourth season."

As he frequently had in the previous year, Robbie's eyes asked Red Hawk a question concerning Jack's graduating in three years.

Red Hawk expected the silent question. "I think we'll have time to get to that part of the story later on, Robbie. I just thought you might enjoy seeing how the brothers came to share the stick. I'll see you soon!"

"Maybe in a month or so," Robbie joked.

THE BEST WAY
TO PUT OUT A FIRE

"Intellectuals solve problems. Geniuses prevent them."

Albert Einstein

Dear Robbie,

Greetings from South Carolina! Jerri and I are back home now and thoroughly enjoyed meeting with you, your parents, your sister, and Jim. It is a great honor to make your acquaintance. Jerri and I are very excited to share in your experience with Red Hawk and your stick.

As I mentioned, I think that I would like to share some things about Jack and my father–especially some of their extensive writings–with you with the hope that you'll get to know them a little better and to see the type of people they were. My father was a prolific reader, writer, and correspondent–he wrote tons and tons of letters. His brother, sisters, nieces, nephews, friends, children, and grandchildren were frequently the recipient of personal notes, letters, photographs, and newspaper clippings annotated as to their particular relevance to them (a dying art, I suspect).

I should make a brief note to emphasize what I consider to be the true significance of these writings. Please remember that before the age of instant worldwide communication capabilities that we enjoy today, most people relied entirely on letters, which frequently took many (often agonizing) days or weeks to exchange. Phone calls were largely unavailable or prohibitively expensive. Also–remember that the World Wide Web, e-mail, You Tube, text messaging, Facebook, Twitter, Facetime, Instagram, and all of the other modern 'social networking' mechanisms are remarkably new in the history of human communication. So, in the days of my father and Uncle Jack (and, obviously before), letters, diaries, scrapbooks, and newspaper articles were, and are now, invaluable historical personal and family documents. Many of us old-timers still yearn for the days of the personal hand-written letter.

So here is one of many letters from my father that I hope to share with you in the coming months and years. I hope you enjoy it as much as I did back in 1946!

My very, very best to you and your family.
"Respect the Game!"
Bruce

Robbie began reading the enclosed letter.

August 30, 1946

Dear Bruce,

My father used to say to us children, "The best way to put out a fire…is to have it not start." Hmmm….seems pretty simple, doesn't it?

Well, as you prepare to enter your freshman year at the Gilman School, let me offer you some thoughts on how you might best maximize your experience there.

Above all things, I beseech you to retain your honor and our family's good name at all costs. Nothing else is even in second place in this regard. Conduct yourself as a gentleman at all times. Stay ahead of–not just 'up with'–your work in all areas. You have shown great promise to date–of which your mother and I are very proud. However, understand that past performance is no guarantee of future success. Therefore, you must be attentive to all of your endeavors with <u>renewed commitment every single day</u>. Nothing less will do in your schooling, professional career, or family responsibilities–nor will it be acceptable.

'The best way to put out a fire is to have it not start,' then, can mean many things. In the literal sense, try to imagine an actual fire sweeping through any structure–such as a house. Picture how difficult it is to contain the fire at any given point– obviously the longer it burns, the more difficult it becomes to extinguish. And also consider the damage inflicted–and the cost to repair that damage (if it is even possible)–that accompanies such destruction.

Now imagine that the fire had not even started and what a tremendous difference you would see. So remember that 'preventing fires' is critical to any home or business.

Now consider a metaphorical application. Think of a problem that you may encounter–say a strain in a friendship, a lapse in judgment of personal behavior, a dishonorable act, etc. Think now of how some of those situations may have been avoided or prevented.

Imagine being on the wrong side of one of these situations and the work and cost that would go into rebuilding the damage you may have caused (and as with a real fire, you may not be able to repair it fully or at all).

Professional firefighters (and people of common sense, it would seem) will tell you that 'fire prevention' is a full-time endeavor. It means to do your very best to establish conditions that do not lend themselves to igniting a fire. Storage of flammable materials far removed from heat sources seems like an obvious good practice.

So seek to cultivate the purest of motives and habits in all regards. Strengthen your mind, body, and spirit so that they will not be susceptible to injury or damage. Identify and hold fast to strong principles–it is these good habits that will protect you, your reputation, your career, and your family in particularly trying times.

To the very best of your ability, you should diligently

practice 'fire prevention' in all areas of your life. Prepare in your academic work so as to not have a 'fire' (a poor or failing grade) on your hands. Cultivate your personal and family relationships with the understanding that you cannot go through this life alone—nor would you want to. You will need help at many turns. People will need help from you. These relationships define who we are and what we are all about.

Develop your athletic skills so that you can react instantly and properly in the heat of a game to help your team succeed.

Stay on top of your financial concerns. You certainly do not want a fire in this area. You will have much to learn about this subject—but like most things, the fundamentals are simple. Be frugal in your spending and save all you can. You will likely be in a constant battle for your entire life to make the best use of your finances. It is never too early to begin to plan properly and exercise good habits.

There is absolutely no substitute for hard work, conscientiousness, and personal responsibility in all areas of your life. Simple. Work at it.

Prevent problems and do not be content to simply fix them. Think and plan ahead. You'll be glad you did.

Your mother and I look forward to your high school years with great eagerness and excitement. Continue to make our family proud.

The best way to put out a fire is to have it not start.

With Love, Pride, and Excitement,

Dad

POLY

"What is a teacher? I'll tell you: it isn't someone who teaches something, but someone who inspires the student to give of her best in order to discover what she already knows."

Paulo Coelho
The Witch of Portobello

RED Hawk visited Robbie on the next full moon, as usual.
"Hi, Robbie," Red Hawk began.

"Hi!" Robbie gushed with his usual excitement.

"Do you have any thoughts on what you might want to see or learn tonight, Robbie?"

"Do you think we can keep learning more about Jack and Doug?"

"I think we can probably do that," Red Hawk responded with a grin. The boys moved through time to 1927.

"Robbie, this is Jack Turnbull's high school, Baltimore Polytechnic Institute—most people just call it 'Poly.' It is April of 1927. There is Jack," Red Hawk gestured. "This is his junior year. He is the captain of the Poly team and they are playing the Naval Academy's 'plebe'—or freshman—team this afternoon.

"His brother Doug is over there in the stands," Red Hawk indicated with his eyes. Robbie looked over with excitement to see Doug. "Jack's coach is giving him some instructions that he hopes Jack will share with the team before they head out to play."

The time travelers listened in on the conversation.

Jack's coach, D. A. Melosh, asked Jack, "So, Jack, how are the guys feeling right now?"

Jack replied with the expected answer, "Great, coach!"

"You sure?"

"What do you mean, coach? The guys are ready to go," Jack insisted.

"O.K., but they just seem a little tense right now–like they don't think they can win. Do you feel that from them?"

"Not really, coach…well, maybe we are a little nervous."

"O.K. Jack, let's make sure that everyone is ready to go. This has always been a big game for us–these midshipmen are very good. I know that we've only beaten them one time in the last fifteen or so years but we have the talent and teamwork to do it again right now."

"Yes, sir."

"We can't play timid out there. We have to be strong everywhere on the field. If we show any sign of weakness or hesitation, they will take advantage of it."

"Yes, sir."

"I can talk to the team all I want, Jack, but it works much better when it comes from leaders like you who will be on the field. So just keep the guys positive no matter what happens out there. There will certainly be a lot of good and bad for us, but we just have to stay focused and play as hard as we can. We've been talking about it all season–haven't we? I know you guys can do a great job with this game."

"Yes, sir."

Jack gathered his team together just before the opening face-off. "Guys, we can do this! Stick together, play hard, and don't ever give up. Navy is probably gonna be really, really physical. But we can do it. Just be ready for it and if we can take some of the body blows and stick checks, we'll be able to put our skill to use. Let's just keep fighting and play as hard as we can."

The team then raised all of their sticks above the huddle.

"On three–Poly!" commanded Jack. "One–two–THREE!"

"POLY!" the boys chanted.

Robbie marveled at how all of the comments and pregame discussions and cheers looked like the ones before his games. The game began with extremely physical play from the midshipmen. It didn't take long for Robbie to notice that they were able to impose their superior physical presence on the younger, less mature high schoolers.

Robbie also couldn't help but notice the difference in the gear the players were wearing. Their sticks were obviously of the old wooden style. They were much bigger and bulkier than his modern plastic and titanium stick. The gloves were big, bulky, and stiff. The helmets the boys were wearing were made of soft leather, with a leather visor, and no facemask. All of the bulk in the playing gear had its effect on the speed–or lack thereof–of play. But Robbie was enthralled none-the-less. He studied the players, their skills, and tactics.

"Stay ahead of the play, boys," Melosh commanded. "Stay ahead of the play."

Robbie asked Red Hawk what Coach Melosh was saying, "Is he saying, 'Stay ahead of the play?'"

"Yes, he is."

"What do you think that means? I don't think any of my coaches have said that."

"Stay ahead of the play," Robbie, "means to know what is going to happen before it happens. Those midshipmen are being pretty physical and knocking some of the Poly boys down or off the play. I think their coach wants them to be more prepared for the contact. He knows they can play well; they are just not ready for how physical Navy is. If they can get past that part, I think they'll be able to do well."

The boys continued to watch. Robbie thought of the many teams that had been particularly physical against his own teams and how it frequently disrupted his team's play.

"Stay ahead, boys. Stay ahead," Melosh continued to implore his team. "You can do it."

Navy scored three goals–all in remarkably similar fashion. A strong body check on a Poly player cradling the ball, followed by a loose ball which was invariably picked up by Navy, followed by a swift upfield pass, followed by two or three more pinpoint passes to an easy shot for a goal. Robbie continued to marvel at how similar it was to his own games despite the fact that the sticks were so big and bulky.

Melosh called a timeout after Navy's third goal to attempt to settle his team and, hopefully, stop the Midshipmen's momentum.

"O.K., boys. Let's settle down a little here. Come on, we talk about this all the time. Remember–CODE. Confidence. Organization. Determination. Enthusiasm. We can get those goals back. We just have to be stronger when we handle the ball. I hope you noticed that they are very happy to body check you." The Poly boys all let out a soft chuckle.

"So if we can slip off those body checks, we should be able to get them out of position and get a good scoring chance. Our skill isn't worth anything if we aren't strong enough to handle the ball! Things work a lot better out there when we have it–so don't let those checks dislodge the ball. If you can hold onto it–you'll be amazed at how much better things will get. Just be ready for the physical play now. Deal with it and do what we do best. Stay ahead of things–don't let them surprise you."

Melosh looked to Jack to reinforce his instructions. "Come on, guys. We can do this. One thing at a time. Let's start with doing a better job with the ball and we'll go from there. Poly on three. One–two–THREE!"

"POLY!" the boys yelled with new conviction.

Robbie and Red Hawk continued to watch the game as Poly was, in fact, able to shake off some of Navy's physical play and control the ball with more strength. Though they still had not been able to score with a few minutes left in the first half, Poly had certainly evened the play and created some new chances to score.

With about a minute left in the half and Navy still up 3–0, Jack received a pass behind the goal and immediately dodged to the front of the goal. Jack's initial move to his right allowed him to slip by his defender enough to cause another Navy defender to attempt to stop him. Jack saw the sliding defender, who was quite a bit bigger than he was, coming in a straight line to stop his dodge. Jack quickly pulled his stick from his right side with an exaggerated sweep across his face to his left as though he would continue his dodge to his left. As the sliding defender was within a step of his intended collision, Jack pulled his stick quickly *back to his right and attempted to side-step the body check. The Navy defender swung his stick violently at Jack's but missed it.*

A face dodge, Robbie thought as he watched.

Jack was hoping that his nifty move would cause the defender to miss his body check as well as his stick check, but he was only partially correct. The defender did not knock him down as he had planned, but he did get a good piece of Jack's chest and left shoulder–almost enough to stop Jack in his tracks. Almost.

Though nearly stopped as his body shuddered, Jack was able to take another step to his right–a hop step actually, while the left side of his body swung around and dragged behind. He quickly regained his balance and realized he had done exactly what his coach had admonished them to do–play with strength through the physical contact. Before his defender could react to Jack's second step, the young Poly attacker drew his stick tight to the right side of his head and rifled a shot past the Navy goalie who never moved. Jack allowed himself a small jump of excitement and tapped the sticks of all of his teammates with his near the goal.

It was the first play all game where a Poly player showed such strength and skill at all–not to mention that close to the goal. All of the Navy defenders near the play stopped and looked at each other in confusion. They had never seen a player do that before–no less a high school player.

Robbie continued to stare on in amazement.

The score remained 3–1 as half-time arrived.

Coach Melosh knew how special Jack's play had been in the context of the game and what it meant to the team, so he allowed Jack to finish the half-time review for the team.

"Guys, come on! We can do this." Jack began. "See how much better we did when we stopped dropping the ball? Just keep fighting."

As play began in the third quarter, Poly continued to hold their own physically. Jack attempted the same move that he had scored on earlier, but this time the sliding Navy defended got more of Jack's body and knocked him to the ground, causing him to drop the ball, which Navy picked up immediately and took to the other end of the field. Jack grinned to himself a little as he got back on his feet, knowing he would have to be a little quicker and stronger on his next dodge.

As time was closing down in the third quarter, Jack made another strong move to the goal, this time eluding his defender so quickly that there was no time for the Navy defense to rotate to help. Jack did a crisp low fake with his stick to draw the goalie down and out of position and firmly placed the ball high into a virtually open net, closing the score to 3–2.

Both teams battled hard through the end of the third and most of the fourth quarters with neither team demonstrating a clear advantage. With about three minutes left in the game, a Navy player attempted a shot that ricocheted off the goal's crossbar all the way to the midfield line. Jack caught his defender napping for just an instant and outraced him to the loose ball. He neatly picked it up on the run and wheeled immediately to attack Navy's goal, leaving his defender about three steps behind. Jack ran directly at a Navy defender stationed about fifteen yards in front of his goal and playing Jack's fellow attackman. With no choice but to prevent Jack from continuing straight to the goal, the defender moved to slow Jack, who deftly threaded the ball to his line mate for an easy shot on goal and a score to tie the game at three each.

Navy called a timeout, which was perfectly fine for Coach Melosh and the Poly team.

"Great job, boys," Melosh began quickly. "Great job! O.K. so now let's just keep doing what we have been doing. Remember CODE! Handle the ball with strength and fight hard on grounders and defense.

"When we get the ball again, they'll probably cheat a little on Jack, so make sure you are all ready to handle the ball.

"Jack, know that they will be coming hard to you and remember that once you have drawn an extra defender or two, there will be people open."

"Yes, sir," Jack nodded.

Jack implored his teammates, "Let's go, guys, keep fighting. Poly on three. One–two–THREE!"

"POLY!"

Navy won the ensuing faceoff and had the ball on offense as time dipped below one minute.

Robbie was trying desperately to see and hear everything that was going on. He could feel the excitement of the crowd, absorbing it all.

Coach Melosh continued his pleas as he paced the sideline. "Keep fighting, boys. Keep fighting! Stay ahead! Stay ahead!"

Jack kept active on the attack end of the field expecting that a ball would come over as it had on Poly's last goal.

Poly's defense was able to frustrate Navy into a disrupted shot that the Poly goalie was able to steer wide of the goal—but which stayed inbounds. Players on both teams fiercely contested the loose ball. A Poly defenseman was the first to get his stick on the ball, but he was immediately driven to the ground by his Navy opponent before he could exercise full control of the ball. He was able, though, to roll the ball up the field toward the midfield line where one of his teammates brilliantly picked it up and began racing toward Navy's end of the field. The crowd all stood and cheered the highschoolers. Robbie's heart raced with excitement as the play unfolded. He knew time was running out.

Coach Melosh patiently allowed his boys to continue the play rather than call for a timeout.

Poly's midfielder raced toward the goal inches in front of a Navy midfielder closing on him. He drew a Navy defenseman to him and spun the ball quickly to Jack who realized that the next defenseman in the rotation was bearing down on him with his usual intention—to break up the play by knocking him down and dislodging the ball. At that instant, while being drilled to the turf, Jack released the ball to his nearside low attackman. As Jack's teammate caught the pass, he encountered another Navy defenseman bearing down on him with the same intention and released the ball across the cage to their third linemate, who caught the ball left handed and "quicksticked" the ball into the goal as he, too, was drilled to the turf by Navy's midfielder who fought gallantly all the way back to his own goal to prevent the shot—but just a fraction of a second late. The only way the now-prone attackers knew that the ball had gone in was by the jump of joy from their teammate who had started the play at midfield. All three attackmen jumped up and met in front of the Navy goal to congratulate each other and then the rest of their teammates as they swarmed in. Time expired anticlimactically a few seconds after the ensuing faceoff.

Robbie was completely overcome with excitement and awe. He turned to Red Hawk, "What a great game. I can't believe how much that looked like one of ours."

"The essence of the game hasn't changed much in many centuries, Robbie." Red Hawk observed.

Each team gathered for a brief team huddle to cheer their opponents. The players lined up and shook hands. When the Navy coach arrived upon Jack, he paused for an extended handshake, "You are quite a young warrior, Jack. Keep working on your game. There is no telling how far you will get."

Though exhausted by his efforts in the game, Jack beamed in pride that an opposing coach had noticed his play and thought well enough of him to tell him—especially a coach from Navy calling him a "warrior."

At the end of each line, the coaches met and agreed that they had never seen a play like Poly's last goal where the players on each side played the situation nearly perfectly. The Poly boys just an inch ahead of the defense when anything less would not have earned them a shot. And the Navy defensemen reacted equally well, tactically, technically, mentally, and physically. To see three attackmen all touch the ball in the span of about two seconds while being knocked down and to maintain their composure to make a such a play was spectacular.

After the brief chat with the Navy coaches, Coach Melosh gathered his Poly players in the corner of the field, as always.

"Boys, that was about as great a game as I have been a part of in twenty years. You played great. You responded to a challenge, met it, and prevailed under difficult circumstances. That's what all of this is all about.

"And as great as it was to win—and it's always great to win—you may want to take a lesson away from this about how incredibly slim margins of victory and defeat are in games like this."

Melosh held up his left hand and pinched his index finger and thumb a fraction of an inch apart. "This much, boys. This much is often the difference between winning and losing, between success and failure. Enjoy the heck out of a great win. But remember that five or six things went our way right at the end there. You certainly made them go your way. But that pipe shot they had could just about as easily gone in. And if any one of those links in that last play are a little off–they might win, just the same. So let's get back to work tomorrow to continue to work on things that give us a chance to continue to make great plays like those."

After Melosh concluded his remarks, the boys all squeezed together for their team cheer led by Jack. "Great job, guys! Let's get back to work tomorrow. Poly on three. One–Two–THREE!"

"POLY!"

Red Hawk moved the scene to the next morning inside the school building at Poly.

Red Hawk began, "Robbie, Coach Melosh was also Jack's trigonometry teacher. So they developed a very strong bond."

The boys watched as Melosh returned test papers from the day before to each of the students. He was meticulous in returning tests–too meticulous for Jack at times. Jack got back an 84. Another "B-"–not what he was hoping for. Melosh watched in pain as Jack stuffed the paper in the back of his notebook before any of his classmates might see it. Jack's brother and sisters had always gotten A's and B's–mostly A's. But Mr. Melosh always rewarded effort–so, despite constant frustration, Jack came for help nearly every day. The grades on Jack's report card always seemed to be a little better than he had calculated. Melosh had a way of making sure his students knew that he was on their side. So Jack and a few others were frequent visitors to Melosh's extra help sessions right after school.

Mr. Melosh walked out of class with a somewhat-dejected Jack, "Jack, I can tell that you are trying hard. I have to tell you that when I was your age, I struggled just about the same amount as you have been.

It didn't keep me from becoming an army officer or from this great job."
Melosh offered with a smile.
  "You are doing a good job. Just keep working."
  "Yes, sir. Thanks."

Robbie thanked Red Hawk for taking him on this trip.

STRING YOUR OWN STICK

"The crafting of each javelin can take months, with sacrifices offered to the shaft of ash or cornel while it still grows on the tree. 'Truth' is the missile weapon's supreme virtue, meaning the absolute straightness of its line, for a warped javelin will not fly true. The javelineers sleep with their spikes: I have seen men wrap them in cloaks while they themselves shiver, to keep the snow and wet from swelling the grain. Each man's dart bears his sign and the sign of his clan; after a fight, he scours the field, retrieving his own and no other's. It is death to do so. A bloodied dart receives its own name, and one which has made a kill is passed down from father to son."

Alexander the Great in
The Virtues of War
Steven Pressfield

CAPTAIN Lewis met Robbie and his parents at Hobart College in Geneva, New York.

Lewis began, "Robbie, John, Mary, this is Rick Gilbert, Hobart College, class of 1974 and Turnbull Award recipient that year."

"It is an honor and pleasure to meet you all. Captain Lewis, thank you for arranging this meeting," Gilbert began.

Lewis added, "I thought you all might want to meet Rick. Rick played at West Genesee High School, about an hour from here in Camillus, New York, right outside Syracuse. They had a pretty darn good team back then—and ever since. They have won a number of

New York state championships and produced an incredible amount of college stars. Same with Hobart–they are considered one of the great programs in history. Rick is still the all-time points leader in NCAA Division II lacrosse with 444 points, with 157 goals and 287 assists."

Gilbert tried to defray his biography, "I got to play with some great players, Jim. My teammates were very good at getting open."

"Well," Lewis continued, "Rick has lived in Florida for quite some time, now, but was planning a trip up here, so I thought it would be good for you all to meet him."

"Rick, I asked Robbie to bring his special stick with him today so that you can take a look at it."

Robbie extended the stick to Rick, "Would you like to look at it, Mr. Gilbert?"

"Love to, Robbie. Please call me Rick, by the way."

Rick accepted the stick and immediately connected with it. Just as Lewis had a year before when he showed Robbie the stick, Rick gently touched the strings and the wood. He spoke to Robbie while almost in a trance.

"Wow, Robbie. This is some stick."

Rick touched every part of every string, the leathers, the twine, and the carvings and writings on the shaft, his eyes never leaving the stick.

Still in his trance, Gilbert continued, "Robbie, did you know that the Native American sticks most likely evolved out of war clubs? If you look particularly at the 'Great Lakes'-type sticks, mostly from tribes like the Ojibwe, you'll see that their small, round pockets look a lot like an old war club. It seems like other tribes evolved off of this model into bigger nets but I have always found it interesting that they seem to have originated in a war club."

After several minutes of studying the stick, Gilbert handed it back to Robbie. "That is the greatest stick I have ever held, Robbie. I grew up playing with the old wooden ones, but transitioned to the plastic during college. I can feel the magic in this one!"

Robbie looked inquisitively as Gilbert had brought two unstrung lacrosse sticks with him. He also laid out four pocket kits, two mesh and two traditional, a small bag with scissors, screwdrivers, knives, and string, and a couple of balls on the table at which they were sitting.

"Robbie, if I could offer you one piece of advice, it would be that you string your own stick. Do you string yours?" Gilbert asked.

"No, sir, I just get at the store and use them the way they are," Robbie confessed.

Lewis smiled as he knew what Rick was about to share.

"Well, Robbie, I think it is pretty important that each player learn to take care of their equipment but particularly their stick. I think it does a lot of good for a player to be that connected with their stick. It says, most of all, that you care. Come on, think about it. Most helmets, shoulder pads, and gloves are pretty much the same. You obviously need to make sure they are in good order, but the fundamental piece of equipment that has its own personality is your stick, isn't it?"

"Yes, sir."

"Your stick is the most critical part of the game. It has to work as well as it possibly can so that your know exactly what it is going to do every time you scoop, dodge, throw, feed, catch, or shoot.

"I remember playing in an important game during my junior year at Hobart, and one of my sidewalls ripped during warm-ups right before the game. I couldn't believe that I had let my stick get to that point. I just hadn't checked it very well. Sidewalls rarely, if ever, 'just rip.' They wear out and fray for several days before they rip. So you can almost always prevent that from happening. In my case, I didn't do it properly. It could have cost my team a lot. Luckily, my backup stick was in pretty good shape. But I got lucky. It should not have gotten to that point.

"So I encourage all young players to take good care of their sticks. Don't rely on other people to take care of your gear. Just about every college team has one or two guys who string and fix most of the sticks. I would discourage that. I think each player should string and maintain their own sticks. The best way to learn is probably to take your backup sticks, tear them down, and then restring them on bus rides and in hotels on the road. It isn't really that difficult to teach yourself.

"I've brought a couple here with me today, Robbie. Here, why don't you take this one and follow what I do with mine?"

Robbie's mind flashed back to his first meeting with Captain Lewis when he described the care that went into their special stick–the Native American warriors whose sweat was on the stings themselves. Though Robbie had heard and understood the importance Lewis conveyed, he had never strung his own stick.

Rick opened the two traditional pocket kits and gave one and an empty head to Robbie.

"If you can follow along with mine, I think you'll see it is pretty easy to do this, Robbie. Wanna try?"

"Sure!"

"O.K., Robbie, let's start by working from the back side of the stick," Rick said as he flipped the stick.

"Just lace the leathers through like this and gently tie them off at the bottom," Gilbert began as he slowly threaded the leather strips through their holes and secured them loosely at the bottom of the head. Robbie did his best to copy Rick as precisely as he could.

Gilbert watched Robbie carefully as his fingers worked almost unconsciously. Lewis sat by quietly, enjoying the lesson, as well.

"Let's get the sidewalls in next, Robbie," Rick demonstrated. Robbie followed, craning his neck here and there to get the proper angle to see Rick's work.

Gilbert talked Robbie through the entire process and shared some stories with him as his fingers worked and massaged the pocket into form.

"It takes a few minutes to weave the stringing in, Robbie. Here just follow what I am doing and I'll help you." Gilbert took the long strand of nylon string and executed perfect loops in and out of the sidewalls and leather strips. Robbie did his best to keep up. When Robbie lagged behind, Gilbert slowed and allowed the boy to catch up.

"You are doing great, Robbie. Looks good!" Gilbert offered.

"Thanks. It's kinda fun."

After they had both woven in all of the nylon stringing, Gilbert told Robbie about the importance of the "shooting strings."

"Every player has their own preference on how to place their shooting strings, Robbie. I liked mine the way I will show you, but you should develop your own preference by experimenting a little," Gilbert offered.

"So let's run the string across the back of your pocket like this," Gilbert demonstrated. "And then just follow mine as I go back across and weave them in."

Robbie continued to keep pace and was beginning to see that he could actually string his own stick!

Gilbert took a ball and squeezed and rolled it into various parts of the pocket and encouraged Robbie to do the same.

"Let's leave the strings just a little loose and throw for a minute," Gilbert suggested.

Robbie and Rick threw for a couple of minutes. Robbie realized that he had just produced the best pocket he had ever used. A nice combination of hold and release.

"O.K., Robbie, let's cut the long pieces off of the strings but leave a little on there in case you need to adjust them. I would cut them only after you use the stick for a few days and are happy with everything.

"That was the hard one, Robbie. Let's try a mesh—it is much easier," Gilbert continued as he opened a mesh kit for each of them. "Go ahead and unstring that one."

Robbie's face conveyed his disappointment in being asked to unravel all of his beautiful work.

It's O.K., Robbie, you know how to do it now," Gilbert consoled as he pulled all of the strings in his stick back out, as well. "O.K., here we go again."

Gilbert talked Robbie through the sequence for the mesh and he was right–it was much easier and faster. As an added bonus, Gilbert showed Robbie how to replace a single sidewall as well as how to extend the life of any part with the convenient use of athletic tape.

"I think after a while your fingers just work those strings naturally. You'll get a pocket and a stick that will work extremely well for you."

Lewis thanked Gilbert for inviting them and providing such a meaningful lesson for Robbie. "That might be the best use of forty-five minutes I have seen in a while, Rick. Thank you."

"Thanks so much for coming, Jim. Robbie–what a great pleasure to meet you! I hope we can stay in touch. I can't or won't presume to tell you what to do or how to play, but I will say that learning how to string your own stick will probably have as much impact on your play as anything else. I hope you keep working on it," Gilbert closed.

"Wow! Thanks, Rick," Robbie gushed.

Twenty-five Big Brothers

"A life is about its events; it's about challenges met and overcome—or not; it's about successes and failures. But more than all of those put together, it's about how we touch and are touched by the people we meet. It's all about the people."

General Colin Powell
It Worked for Me

RED Hawk came to Robbie on the next full moon.

"Hi Robbie," Red Hawk greeted his friend. "How 'bout I pick a place to go tonight?"

"That would be great," Robbie eagerly agreed. "Where?"

"Well, last month we saw Jack playing at Poly. That was a pretty good game, wasn't it?" Red Hawk smiled with his understatement.

"I'll bet you didn't know that the next two years—1928 and 1929—Jack played for the great Mount Washington Club team, one year while he was still at Poly and the next spring after he had actually graduated from Poly but was not yet enrolled at Johns Hopkins."

Robbie offered Red Hawk a baffled look.

"It is a bit of a long story, Robbie. But we should probably talk about it and take a look. The time that Jack spent with Mount Washington those two springs really defined him as a player and a person. Try to imagine a player coming out of high school today, going straight to Major League Lacrosse for two years, and then returning to college after that experience. Think of how much better, stronger, and more mature a

player would be upon returning to college. That is comparable to what Jack did."

Robbie still stared back in total confusion, unable to imagine the circumstances that might have led to that situation. *"I'd love to hear that story."*

"O.K., well to begin with, Jack started at Poly a year before he probably should have. He did O.K. with his grades, but certainly not great. As Jack struggled more and more as he went along, his parents asked the school to hold him back one grade so he could catch up.

"Then he lost his eligibility for his senior year due to the fact that he had played four seasons already. And then he graduated in February so he was no longer enrolled and, obviously, could not play that year either."

This was all new to Robbie.

Red Hawk continued, *"Jack always said that his coaches and teammates had the greatest impact on his life. As I hope you'll see, his teammates at Mt. Washington took him under their wings and really helped him. His brother Doug was on the team, which also had a huge impact on him. One player, the team captain, Oster 'Kid' Norris, though, became Jack's mentor in every respect. But what really happened was that Jack ended up with about twenty-five big brothers on that team.*

"Let's look a little at the Mt. Washington-Crescent game, O.K?"

"That would be great!" Robbie said eagerly.

"The Crescent Club is from Brooklyn, New York, Robbie. They are one of the best teams in the country and have had a great rivalry with the Wolfpack for many years. There are Jack and Doug," Red Hawk pointed to each. The game had just begun.

After Jack's first pass, he was knocked to the ground with a high and late body check by a Crescent defender, which was not called as a foul by the officials–though it clearly should have been. Doug noticed the cheap shot on his brother but was prepared to let it go for now. Kid Norris, as captain of the team, was not nearly as ready to ignore it and approached the offender.

"What was that?" Norris yelled.

"What was what?" the defender snapped back.

"That was a bad hit. Come on, you should know better than that. And he is a high schooler right now. We don't need that garbage."

"If he is in high school, maybe he shouldn't be out here."

Norris started to respond but simply walked away from the discussion, knowing any further comments would be of no use.

Doug stood by quietly knowing that Jack would be up to the physical challenge and had actually become a bit amused by the discussion. He also knew that the next time Norris had an opportunity to 'communicate' with this defender, it would likely be with a body check. It didn't take long for Norris' opportunity.

Just a couple of minutes later, the defender had just picked up a loose ball near Norris, who took the opportunity to pay back the hit on Jack. Norris delivered a rock-solid chest-to-chest hit that not only dropped his opponent—the first point of contact as the Crescent defender hit the ground being his shoulder blades—but caused him to drop the ball—and his stick. Mount Washington gladly picked up and attacked the goal.

Robbie felt himself cringe—and chuckle a little—as he watched.

As play continued on, Robbie counted no less than six jarring body checks on the same Crescent player by different Mount Washington players who had taken Norris' lead. Norris added one more 'reminder' toward the end of the game after the outcome on the scoreboard had long-since been decided. Robbie noticed that all of the hits were perfectly legal and well placed but had certainly made a point.

In between the collisions on the Crescent defender, Robbie studied both Jack and Doug. He had never seen Doug play in his visits with Red Hawk. Though maybe not quite as flashy as Jack, Doug was incredibly steady. Robbie noticed the little things that Doug was doing so well. He picked up five or six loose balls by simply being in the right place at the right time. Doug's efforts on his team's rides—defending on the attack end of the field when his team had lost the ball—were exemplary. His stickwork and footwork were as clean and crisp as Robbie had ever seen.

Robbie also noticed Doug contributing in a different way in support of Jack. He simply raced by the defender who had offended Jack—three *times in a row, almost mocking him with the ease in which he did it, and scoring each time.*

Jack was able to tally two goals and Doug went about his business by totaling four. The Mount won 9–5, though the score was an afterthought to the real story, which was the way that Jack's teammates backed him up physically. There were no more cheap shots on Jack in that game or any others the rest of the season.

"You know, Robbie," Red Hawk offered, "Jack told me in one of my visits that the support he received from his teammates in that game was the highlight of his lacrosse career. For such a young player to have earned such respect from a world-class team like that–and it had nothing to do with being Doug's brother and everything to do with himself–it meant the world to him and cemented his confidence on the field for the rest of his career.

"Kid Norris, who was the first one to stick up for him, played and coached at Mount Washington for thirty years! So he remained an active part of Jack's life for about fifteen years after this. The field where the team now plays, by the way, is named in Kid's honor. From all I have learned about him, I think all of his teammates, coaches, and players will tell you that he had a tremendously positive impact on their careers–not the least of whom was Jack. Kid was inducted into the National Lacrosse Hall of Fame in 1962. Some of the other guys on that team played for many years, as well. So the Mount Washington Club team was a bedrock of Jack's life. He went from being a ball boy when he was little, to a star even while in high school, and then returned as a superstar after his three years at Hopkins. He loved playing with that team and those players and coaches."

"Three years at Hopkins? Don't most players go for four?" Robbie asked.

"Three years–that's right. We'll get to that part later," Red Hawk teased.

"There is one other piece of 1928 that I think I should mention, Robbie," Red Hawk continued. "The organizers for the Olympic Games in Amsterdam decided to add lacrosse as a demonstration sport. General

Douglas MacArthur, the head of the American Olympic Committee, formed a group to determine the team to represent the United States. He established a playoff format between Mt. Washington, Navy, Rutgers, Johns Hopkins, and the University of Maryland.

"Mount Washington was undefeated going into the Olympic qualification tournament and played Hopkins at Baltimore Stadium in front of about 9,000 fans but lost 6-4. Hopkins later beat Maryland to earn the Olympic berth. They went on to play in front of huge crowds in Amsterdam and ended up with the best overall record based on goal differentials!

"You know that Jack competed in the 1932 and 1936 Olympics. He was pretty close to being there in 1928 also! So, I hope you would agree that 1928 was probably the most important year in Jack's career in just about every respect."

Robbie nodded in agreement.

"I'll see you soon, Robbie," Red Hawk closed.

"Thanks, Red Hawk. See you soon!"

You Are What Your Performance Says You Are

"We don't talk very much."
Navy SEAL Commanding Officer

Robbie,
    I hope all is well. I like this letter from my father–hope you enjoy it, as well.
    My best to you and your family.
               "Respect the Game!"
               Bruce

Robbie opened the enclosed letter.

June 6, 1957

Dear Bruce,
    Congratulations on your graduation from West Point! Your mother and I are extremely proud of you and this tremendous accomplishment.
    I know that I have shared a number of my father's sayings with you. Well, here is another one that you may want to remember as you head off to lead soldiers in defense of our country, **"You are what your performance says you are."** I think this one is about as simple as it can be. In short–talk is

cheap. You can talk all you want about doing things but if you haven't *done* them, then it is only talk.

As I have confessed to you during your journey to and through West Point, I cannot claim to have first-hand experience in the ways of the military. But, please remember that I have found many remarkable similarities in my business experience. Some would even argue that leadership in the civilian sector might be *more* difficult than in a number of military settings. I can assure you that every one of my employees looks at me in the exact same way that your troops will look at you. So please take these thoughts to heart–I think they are largely universal.

I suspect that the soldiers under your purview will be watching you like a hawk. Every single thing you do–key word *do*–will be heavily scrutinized by your troops. They will know when your actions match your words and when they will not. To be sure, you will need to speak, write, and communicate clearly. And you should work hard on these aspects of your leadership skills. When I say that talk is cheap–that is true. But, at the same time, it is critical to communicate your thoughts effectively. Then, as you put your words into actions, the true value of what you have said will come to life. There is a time and a place–a critical time and place–for clear talk. But none of your talk with be worth your bars if you can't 'walk the talk.' Do the work. Be the first one there and be the last to leave. Be there for your soldiers. Don't talk about being there for them. Don't talk about why you were not there–be there.

Good leaders don't just direct people to do things–they *explain* why that task is necessary and important. Once a person understands *why* they are doing something, they are much more likely to *want* to do it–and do it well. That, I think, is true leadership.

As I have told you and your brothers and sisters many times, it should be painfully clear to every person with whom you come in contact that you are the product of a strong family and an excellent education. Certainly not in an elite, haughty way, but in a warm, gracious, caring, hardworking, intelligent, and strong way. Your soldiers should be able to tell from the first minute that they meet you that you will be the kind of officer they want, need, and *deserve*.

There was rarely any time when we children did not know where we stood in our father's eyes. He expected us to be polite, courteous, gracious, hardworking, and tough-minded. When we displayed any deficiency in these areas or talked about why we hadn't accomplished a specific task, he addressed us quickly, firmly, and positively. It seems to me that this would be a good way to engage your soldiers.

Our father always preached performance, performance, performance. "Get the job done. Don't *talk about* getting the job done. *Get* the job done."

Jack wrote to us frequently about the difficulties and challenges he and his men faced in the War. I know for a fact that he was able to lead his airmen as effectively as he did because of the lessons our father taught him.

I think Jack would tell you to work hard on your relationships with your soldiers and to take good care of them. He would tell you to not underestimate the importance of your material readiness, train hard, teach your soldiers to execute under duress, build a Team Ethos within your unit, and bring a positive attitude every day.

You certainly can't be a good officer without being a good person. It will require intense work and dedication to continue to learn, improve, and grow in the ways that you will need and want to–but your soldiers will deserve–and appreciate–your very best.

I know that you are capable of excelling in the future as you have to this point. However, I suspect that West Point was the easy part. Get ready to really work.

You are what your performance says you are.

With Love and Pride,

Dad

FOOTBALL & HOCKEY

"Never try to teach a pig to sing. It wastes your time and annoys the pig."

sign in the office of former
Pittsburgh Penguins (NHL) Coach
Bob Johnson

R ED Hawk visited Robbie again on the next full moon.
"Robbie, how about we take a little different look at Jack this time?"

"Sure. What do you mean?"

"Well, we haven't talked too much about Jack's other sports–but he was All-State in football when he was at Hopkins, and he also played ice hockey, you know. How 'bout we look at some of that?"

"Great!"

Red Hawk began the scene a few minutes before kickoff at a Hopkins football game in 1931. He began to share a little history with Robbie, who was clearly excited to be there.

"There is Jack," Red Hawk pointed. "He plays halfback and defensive back for the Hopkins football team. They have not been particularly strong the last couple years–but Jack has really helped them improve from 1-8 his freshman year to where they are this year, 5-2, going into this last game. Jack led the state in scoring a couple of years ago and was selected All-State.

As play began, Jack received the opening kickoff and returned it about thirty yards. As Robbie had experienced on some of his other trips, he found himself spellbound by Jack in his playing days, as well as by the uniforms and equipment (or lack thereof) of the players. Robbie smiled at the baggy pants, high black shoes, small shoulder pads, long-sleeve padded jerseys, and facemask-less leather helmets.

Robbie's heart raced with excitement as Hopkins huddled for their first play. Red Hawk offered, "I think Jack really enjoyed the variety of sports he played. He worked very, very hard on each one, but the variety kept things fresh for him. I think so many boys your age are starting to just focus on one sport. Is that a fair statement?"

Hopkins broke the huddle and set their formation. Robbie was amazed by the formation and stances of all of the players. Jack received a pitch out wide to the right and immediately turned upfield. Jack wiggled past the first two would-be tacklers and then slammed into the last two as he was being driven out of bounds. Robbie noted that Jack gained about twelve yards—pretty nice run.

After giving the previous question some thought while Hopkins huddled, Robbie replied, "I think that's true. A lot of my friends keep saying they want to just play lacrosse. They say they will train all fall and all winter just for the spring and summer seasons. They play on club teams and travel so far away. Do you think I should I do that to get better?"

Red Hawk sat quietly smiling. He had seen this change just in the past decade. He advised, "Robbie, I think you should play a few sports for as long as you can. You learn so much more that way."

"Really?" Robbie questioned.

"Definitely. Watch Jack."

On the next play Jack took another pitch but to the other side this time. Again Jack slipped through the first couple of tacklers, ending up with about an eight yard gain.

"Did you just see how Jack used his eyes and shoulders to fake those defenders trying to tackle him?" Red Hawk asked.

"That quick little fake?"

"Yes. That perfect amount of hesitation to bait his defender into

biting right, then taking off to the left," Red Hawk explained. "You can learn so much from playing multiple sports. Your skills complement each other as they transfer from one field onto the next. The basics of the games are the same. The only thing that really changes is the equipment."

"That was like a split dodge!" Robbie realized.

"Sure was," Red Hawk agreed.

The boys continued to watch Jack grind out sizeable yardage on every carry until his team scored. Robbie noticed that Jack was never brought down by the first tackler—and usually not even the second or third.

Conversely, when Jack was in the defensive backfield, he didn't miss a tackle. What a joy to watch, Robbie thought.

Red Hawk continued, "I think you can see that Jack had a lot of natural football skill, but I think he has also learned so much from playing all of his sports. I think the strength and toughness that he has worked on in football translated very well to lacrosse and hockey. I think the skill and finesse that he has developed in lacrosse and hockey has helped him out here in football. They all work together. All of the sports require strength, skill, toughness, and teamwork.

"I'd like to quickly show you one more thing tonight, Robbie. Is that alright?" Robbie stared at Red Hawk with a quick nod of approval.

The scene quickly changed and suddenly the boys were inside a chilly hockey arena close by in Baltimore. "Amateur Hockey League" read a sign on the boards near the middle of the rink. In order to play games, Hopkins sometimes had to play against Baltimore's semi-professional team.

Red Hawk and Robbie sat in the cramped bleachers near Jack's bench quite a bit before the scheduled game time. Jack always got to the rink earlier than expected to try to hone his stick and skating skills, which were slightly below the level of his more-experienced comrades. The small stick he played with was held easily in one hand, and his muscle and speed helped him compensate on the ice-particularly on loose pucks and defense, but Jack always sought to improve his skills.

Jack began circling the rink, slowly at first to warm up. But he quickly increased his pace and began a series of challenges. He first worked on his skating—practicing his starts and stops, changes of directions, and skating backwards. The only other person in the rink was the manager who had opened it early to allow Jack some ice time. Jack worked and worked on his skating.

After about thirty minutes of just skating, Jack took his stick from the bench and scattered several pucks around the rink. He then, systematically, began working on his stick handling, racing between the blue lines simply handling the puck. He worked on his wrist shot—taking at least one hundred. Then on to his slap shot—another one hundred or so.

By now Jack's teammates and their opponents began to straggle into the locker rooms. Jack continued to work. Now he mixed up the skills, skating and shooting together. Frontward, backwards, weaving in and out of imaginary defenders, stopping, starting, passing pucks off the boards to himself, shooting.

Jack took a short break right before his teammates began to make their way onto the ice and then he joined them for their normal warm-up. Robbie guessed that Jack had done about an hour's worth of practice on his own.

"He does that a lot," Red Hawk shared, familiar with Jack's routine.

The boys continued to watch as the game began. Though Jack was clearly not the smoothest skater, passer, or shooter on his team, Robbie could feel the intensity Jack brought to his team. His tenacity, effort, and athleticism were evident. On every shift, it seemed Jack threw a strong body check on an opponent, which made them think twice about trying to slip by Jack again.

Jack's shifts—he played defense—looked remarkably similar throughout the game—strong, aggressive, and effective all night. He gathered in a number of loose pucks by sheer will. Though Hopkins lost the game 4-1, Robbie and Red Hawk could see Jack's team's play actually pick up every time he was on the ice. His mere presence seemed to inspire his comrades.

"I hope you enjoyed that, Robbie. Though Jack was obviously one of the all-time greats in lacrosse, he took an equal amount of pride in his *football and hockey pursuits—and derived a great deal from doing all three," Red Hawk closed. "We better go."*

"Wow! Thanks, again, for another great trip, Red Hawk," Robbie beamed. With that, Red Hawk waved goodbye for the month.

STAR FLAGS

"You have to be thankful and lead your life in a way that people can look to it as an example."

Mark Johnson
Former NHL and Team USA hockey star
Head Coach, University of Wisconsin Women's Hockey Team

ROBBIE and his parents met Captain Lewis once again at the Mount Washington Tavern in Baltimore. The last time they gathered there, Lewis and Robbie's family met with Stewart McLean, U.S. Naval Academy, Class of 1946 and the first recipient of the Turnbull Award. This time they gathered to meet Bob Scott.

Lewis handled the honors. "Robbie, John, Mary, Catherine, I'd like you to meet Mr. Bob Scott."

The group all shook hands and made their way to a table for lunch.

"Robbie, Coach Scott played at Johns Hopkins and, after some time in the army, was later the head coach there for twenty years and then Director of Athletics for another fifteen. He coached some great teams and players at Hopkins—though we were somehow able to beat them three times while I was at Navy," Lewis offered a smile at Coach Scott.

"That was a tough stretch for us, Jim," Coach Scott conceded.

Lewis continued, "Coach Scott is a member of the National Lacrosse Hall of Fame and widely considered as one of the greatest coaches the game has seen. Beyond that, I must say from knowing him for all these years, everyone who has ever interacted with him will tell you that you will never meet a finer gentleman."

Scott sat modestly as Lewis regaled his guests but then politely steered the conversation toward the family.

"Thanks, Jim, but I think our lunch here today is about Robbie and his family."

The Joneses immediately felt the warmth and sincerity that Coach Scott exuded. "Robbie, it is a great honor and privilege to be with you and your family today. I understand from Captain Lewis that you are now in possession of a very special lacrosse stick. I have to tell you that I knew nothing of this stick until very recently when Jim called me to arrange this meeting. Can you tell me a little bit about it?"

"Yes, sir. Well, the stick has belonged to several people over the last two-hundred-and-fifty years or so, beginning with a Native American named Red Hawk. Captain Lewis passed the stick along to me about a year and a half ago. I have it here in this bag, if you would like to see it."

Scott beamed in delight as he listened to Robbie's story. "I would love to see it!"

Robbie slipped the stick from its leather bag and gently handed it to Mr. Scott, who stood, as if greeting a person, to receive it. Just like all of the previous stewards, Scott's eighty-four-year-old hands tingled as he held it.

Scott slowly sat back down, still holding the stick. Robbie continued, "The carvings on the shaft were done by the previous stewards." Scott pulled out his reading glasses to inspect the carvings.

"And I have been able to *meet* with Red Hawk…," the boy paused as he saw Coach Scott look up at him with great curiosity. Robbie took his cue from his parents and Lewis to continue, "… in my dreams on each full moon…and he has taken me to places…to see some of the history of the stick and the people who have had it."

"Well, I'll be darned!" Scott exclaimed. "In all the years I have been involved with the game, this is the most amazing thing I have ever heard." He looked at Lewis in utter amazement. "So you were the steward before Robbie, Jim?"

"Yes, sir, and it's all true, Coach," Lewis confirmed. "Very few people know of the story of this stick and its magnificent powers."

"Well, thanks for including me in that group. Why would you share this with me?" Scott asked.

"I thought it might be helpful for Robbie to meet you because you know quite a bit about the person who passed the stick to me in 1959," Lewis teased with knowing eyes.

"In the last eighteen months or so Robbie has learned quite a bit about the stick—but there is still so much more to know. I think you can help him a lot."

Scott's mind was trying to process all of what he had just heard. He looked at Robbie, "Do you know who presented the stick to Captain Lewis, son?"

Scott braced himself.

"Yes, sir.... Doug Turnb..."

"*Doug Turnbull?*" Scott yelled as he nearly jumped out of his chair even before Robbie had said the full name. "Son of a gun! I knew Doug for fifty years!"

The table erupted in laughter.

"Son of a gun! Son of a gun! Jim, this is too incredible. Doug never gave even a hint of this story to me. How is all of this possible?"

"It's all true, sir," Lewis coughed out over his laugh of delight.

After Coach Scott caught his breath and regained his bearings, Lewis nodded to Robbie. The boy took Lewis's cue to continue and began to add softly as to ease yet another assault on Scott's sensibilities.

"Doug's brother Jack also shared the stick with him—so I have gotten to *meet* both of them through Red Hawk."

Scott howled again. "Jack, too? I'll be darned! Son of a gun!" The table erupted yet again, drawing the attention of nearly everyone in the tavern.

Lewis took over shortly, "Coach, Robbie, his family, and I attended Hopkins' first home game last year and observed the 'Flag' ceremony. I know that you had the honor of attaching those flags to the nets in 1952 and obviously participated in nearly every one since. Perhaps you could share with us what that ceremony means to you and maybe something about the players represented on the flags, themselves."

"Well, Robbie, it is an incredibly meaningful ceremony for us here at Hopkins. Jim told me that we might be discussing this topic– so please allow me to refer to some notes I brought," Scott began as he pulled a set of index cards from his blazer pocket.

"Well, son, the ceremony began in 1919 when 'Father Bill' Schmeisser, the coach at the time, asked the school to offer a tribute to the Hopkins players who had fallen in World War I. One of them, First Lieutenant W. Brown Baxley, Engineering School Class of '17 was the brother of the captain of the 1919 team, Herb Baxley. Lieutenant Baxley was a member of the American Expeditionary Forces in France and died in the line of duty on August 1, 1918.

"We've held the ceremony every year since. And, yes, I had the honor of placing the flags on in 1952. I've been privileged to do many things in this great game including winning a number of national championships, coaching some truly dedicated and talented young men, and meeting thousands of wonderful people, but placing those memorial flags on our nets my senior year was probably the most memorable for me. I had chills going through my body the whole time. Remember that the pain and suffering that we all endured in World War II was still raw in everyone's hearts and minds.

"My daughter was able to help me find some information on these men. We are planning to follow up on some of this information.

"What we were able to find was that in addition to LT Baxley, another player who died World War I was Army Second Lieutenant Warren B. Hunting who died on July 15, 1918 in France. He held a Ph.D. degree and had written–but not yet published–a book when he passed–so his family had it published posthumously. He is buried at the Aisne-Marne American Cemetery in Belleau, France.

"We also learned that Edmund 'Ted' Prince died in the Battle of Montfaucon in France in September of 1918. Ted was a graduate of Towson High School, which is not too far from here, Class of 1911 and then Hopkins, Class of 1915. The Towson High Alumni Association website had the rest of this information: After Hopkins, he entered Virginia Theological Seminary where he was ordained an Episcopal minister in 1917. He left the Seminary, enlisted in the U.S. Army as a private to fight in World War I, and later attained the rank of Lieutenant. Towson High School believes that Ted was its only student or graduate to die in World War I. Towson High presents a memorial scholarship in Ted's name each year. This award is given 'to a senior who, in addition to being a good student, possesses characteristics of heart, mind and conduct as evidenced by a spirit of loyalty and service to Towson High.'

"What a special way to remember someone, don't you think?" Scott paused and looked at Robbie's mother.

"The best way," she said softly.

Robbie and his family continued to sit in rapt attention.

Scott paused before he was to begin his World War II list, "It would seem that you have learned quite a bit about Jack Turnbull, then?" he questioned Robbie.

"Yes, sir. Quite a bit."

"Well, I had several cards of information here on Jack," Scott paused with a smile, knowing that he had been mildly tricked by Lewis. "So we won't need that part right now, Jim?"

"No, sir."

"O.K., well, in addition to Jack, then," Scott resumed, moving the note cards related to Jack aside, "the World War II casualties included Army Captain Frank Cone. This is from another website: According to family records, in 1941, while living in Houston, Frank's Army Reserve unit was called into active duty and he was sent to the Philippines, arriving in Manila in November, 1941. He was a medical doctor attached to the 26th Cavalry or Philippine Scouts, a mounted cavalry unit at Fort Stotsenberg. He was later reassigned to the 86th Field Artillery. After the start of World War II, American forces withdrew to the Bataan Peninsula where Frank was assigned to field hospital #2. He was surrendered on April 9, 1942, along with the other U. S. forces on Bataan, participated in the Bataan Death March, and died a Prisoner of War of the Japanese on September 3, 1942 in Cabanatuan #1 prison camp. His grave is in the Philippines.

"It seems that Major David H. W. Houck was 'executed' by the Japanese after a sham trial in 1945. After his plane was shot down and he was captured, he was accused of bombing a civilian ship in Hong Kong Harbor. Though he did not have legal representation in the brief trial, he was found guilty of war crimes and was executed by a firing squad the next day. A judge later overturned the finding of the original court," Scott closed with a soft groan as if to emphasize the futility of the eventual finding.

"According to findagrave.com, Walter J. Fahrenholz enlisted in the Army Air Corps Feb 1, 1943 in Panama City, Florida and later became a member of the 430th Fighter Squadron, 474th Fighter Group of the U.S. Army Air Force. He died November 18, 1944, and is buried in Mount Olivet Cemetery in Baltimore. He was awarded the Purple Heart."

He continued. "It seems that George D. Penniman coached Johns Hopkins University lacrosse for a couple years, and his grandfather helped start the football program there. We'll have to do some more work on his story.

"We were able to determine that Army Second Lieutenant Edward A. Marshall served in the 51st Infantry Battalion, 4th Armored Division and died on November 10, 1944. He was awarded the Silver Star, Bronze Star, and Purple Heart. He is buried in the Lorraine American Cemetery in St. Avold, France."

"I have become particularly pained by the loss of Army Captain Pete Reynolds, JHU '34. Pete was a standout on the Hopkins football team as well as an All-American in lacrosse. He was a member of the '32 Hopkins Olympic lacrosse team. He was the head football coach at his alma mater, Mount St. Joseph's in Baltimore, and an Army Reserve officer when he was called to active duty in January of 1941. He later served in the Philippines. When the United States surrendered on the Bataan Peninsula, Captain Reynolds apparently survived the Bataan Death March.

"It seems that Pete was being transported from the Philippines probably to a slave labor camp in Japan on an old Japanese freighter—which became known as 'Hell ships'—when the ship was struck by an allied torpedo. So Pete and his comrades likely perished under 'friendly fire' after having survived some of the most horrific treatment of the war. What a shame and tremendous loss. Pete is remembered today, along with Jack, with the Turnbull-Reynolds Trophy, symbolic of exceptional sportsmanship and leadership within the Hopkins lacrosse program. It has been presented all these years by the Class of '32—I think Church Yearley was the last surviving member of that Olympic team and came to the Hopkins awards dinner right up until he passed away.

"We also lost one of my players in Vietnam, Chuck Aronhalt, class of '64, who, Captain Lewis has informed me, you learned about earlier. Chuck was a great player for us—as well as for the Hopkins football team. He died in heroic ground action in Vietnam, for which he posthumously received the Distinguished Service Cross. If you will indulge me, I'd like to read the citation on Chuck's DSC."

Scott unfolded a piece of paper and began, "This is still difficult for me. Sorry,

"The President of the United States takes pride in presenting the Distinguished Service Cross (Posthumously) to Charles E. Aronhalt, Jr., First Lieutenant (Infantry), U.S. Army, for extraordinary heroism in connection with military operations involving conflict with an armed hostile force in the Republic of Vietnam, while serving with Company B, 1st Battalion,

8th Infantry, 1st Brigade, 4th Infantry Division. First Lieutenant Aronhalt distinguished himself by exceptionally valorous
actions on 18 May 1967 while serving as platoon leader during
a search and destroy mission in Pleiku Province. When another
platoon of his company received devastating fire, Lieutenant
Aronhalt requested that his platoon be sent to aid the stricken
unit. As he led his men forward, however, the entire company
began receiving intense fire from numerous concealed positions.
Lieutenant Aronhalt tried to pull his men back, but they were
unable to leave their cover. Since the platoon couldn't maneuver
in any direction, he positioned his machine guns to strengthen
the unit's defensive posture. He tried to form a perimeter,
but was prevented by the hostile fire sweeping his positions.
Seeing several wounded men, Lieutenant Aronhalt again tried
to move his men forward. Unable to do this, he personally
fought his way through the intense crossfire and began pulling
the wounded to safety. He repeatedly entered the exposed area
and fought his way out with wounded men over his shoulder.
Seeing that casualties were mounting faster than he could carry
them out, he stood up and charged the insurgents alone. His
rifle jammed as he ran, but he picked up a machine gun and
continued charging and firing steadily to give his men a chance
to withdraw. Lieutenant Aronhalt was mortally wounded in the
successful attempt at drawing the fire from his men. His valiant
actions prevented the Viet Cong from taking the lime of any
one of his men."

Scott groaned softly as he finished Chuck's citation–the pain
was still there. He took a breath to finish,

"First Lieutenant Aronhalt's extraordinary heroism and devo-
tion to duty, at the cost of his life, were in keeping with the
highest traditions of the military service and reflect great credit
upon himself, his unit, and the United States Army."

As the group finished their lunch, Coach Scott thought it might be a good idea for his new friends to see the actual 'Star Flags' and invited the group to accompany him to Homewood Field.

As they arrived, they saw a few Hopkins players on the field working on their shooting on the flagless goals, which were strung with worn, tattered, grey nets. Quite different than game day! Scott's group lingered at the side of the field and admired the extra work the boys were putting in.

The hallowed flags were kept in the new Cordish Center for safekeeping and Coach Scott knew exactly how to get to them. He took his group to this little-known and even less-accessed place and carefully reached for the flags. He held them lightly above his flat, upward facing palms and explained the stars on each of them. Robbie's eyes twinkled as he studied the cloth and embroidery that made up each one. The stars were much larger up close, but they still remained a very small tribute to the sacrifices these men and their families made for the United States.

As the boy studied the two rows of matching stars, one particular star caught the soft light in a slightly different way than the others and radiated its warmth to him. Robbie immediately felt a special connection with *that* star. Though there was no indication that any one star was designated for a specific fallen hero, he *knew* it was Jack's.

The boy asked Coach Scott if he could hold the flag. As soon as he touched the star, Robbie felt as one *with* Jack. For the first time in his amazing journey, Robbie felt directly connected with Jack. He could *feel* him in the star. The history, power, and majesty of all that he had learned from his stick was seeping into his fingers at that very second. A sense of connection, respect, and gratitude overtook Robbie in a way that he had never experience before. The boy was long past the point when he unsure that his connections to Red Hawk and the rest of the stewards of the stick were even possible. He was sure for quite some time that they were real, but he *knew* it now–and this experience added one more brick in the foundation that would help him through his life.

Robbie looked up and locked his eyes with Lewis', who held the boy's eyes ever so slightly, indicating to Robbie that Lewis was experiencing the *exact* same connection with the *exact* same star at that *exact* same second and served as a reminder for Robbie to know that he was not alone on this journey.

As Coach Scott placed the flags back in their place, he thanked all of his guests for including him in their journey and offered Robbie and his parents all of his contact information.

"I hope we'll be able to stay, in contact," he said with genuine sincerity.

"Me, too!" agreed Robbie.

'CALLING'

"I don't know shi*!"
Realization arrived upon by a U.S. Navy commander
shortly after entering a National War College master's
degree program, following a tour as commanding officer
of a nuclear powered, nuclear missile-capable submarine

ON the next full moon, Red Hawk took Robbie just west of
Baltimore to Rutherford Air Field in June 1931.

*It was a bright, sunny day at the airfield as Red Hawk began his
description for Robbie. "There is Jack with his instructor pilot, Jack
Carroll. Jack has just completed his junior year at Hopkins. His instructor is a Hopkins alumnus a few years ahead of him."*

*The boys listened in on the discussion. The instructor began, "Jack,
it is great having you here. I can tell how excited you are for this first
lesson and I think you are going to really enjoy this challenge. It is right
in line with your natural abilities and the traits that have helped you be
successful on the field—strength, courage, focus, skill, and determination.
All of these will be tested in the next few months and will be critical in
earning your proficiency.*

*"I had the good fortune to fly for the Army Air Corps for several
years and I hope to be able to share some of that training and experience
with you.*

"Before we officially begin our training next week, we'll need to do

some 'ground school' first. But for today, how 'bout we just go up and see how it feels? I'll fly," Carroll said with a wink.

"Great!" said Jack.

"O.K. Let's get on up there, then."

Carroll walked Jack slowly around the plane conducting a number of pre-flight checks to make certain that the plane was ready to go and then climbed into the cockpit. After another series of check offs, Carroll started the engines.

Jack could feel his pulse increase with each passing minute. Without ever flying before, he knew that this was what he was meant to do—his 'calling.'

After several more checks, Carroll allowed the plane to accelerate down the runway and lifted it softly into the air. The exhilaration of becoming airborne struck Jack with full force. Though his instructor was doing the actual flying, Jack immediately envisioned himself at the controls.

"Focus on little things, Jack. They make all the difference," Carroll pointed out after they had leveled off.

Carroll banked the plane softly back and forth to allow Jack to acclimate to the sky.

"Always stay a few seconds ahead, Jack. Don't take anything for granted up here. Things can get pretty bad pretty quickly. You can get real stupid real fast up here. So please don't ever think you know as much as you'll need. This will be a life-long process," Carroll continued.

"You must always stick to your fundamentals. When things get difficult or you have to work through a problem, you will revert back to the skills you have practiced the most. So everything we work on up here must be executed as perfectly as possible every single time. It is the only way to prepare for difficulties."

Carroll rocked the plane a little more heavily. Jack responded instinctively not with fear or discomfort but with a calculation of what his reaction with the controls would be. Carroll noticed Jack reacting in this manner and knew that Jack was born to fly. A number of Carroll's other students were simply not cut out for this challenge and he would gently but firmly counsel them into another pursuit.

Jack knew the challenges and risks. But, as Carroll had pointed out, he yearned for this challenge. After his sessions with his instructor, he would be on his own to succeed or fail–alone. He soaked in every second of his time in the air and every word Carroll offered.

"We'll work on all of the skills you'll need, Jack. Don't worry about that. I'll do my best to help you. Your job will be to learn as much as you can and work at improving every time we go up. It won't be too long before you are ready–trust me," Carroll said confidently. "But never forget that you'll never stop learning how to be a good pilot. I still learn things up here all the time. O.K., here, I'll let you take control for a few minutes."

Jack did not hesitate when Carroll announced, "O.K. You've got it! Just keep 'er steady and smooth. Keep an eye on your needle and keep it in the center."

Jack looked at the needle indicating the disposition of his wings. Centered meant flat, which meant good.

"Things are much easier on a nice clear day like today, Jack. But when it is cloudy and you lose some visibility, you will rely on your needle to keep your orientation," Carroll noted.

"Go ahead and rock it a little," Carroll instructed. "Watch what your needle does when you bank."

Jack followed the instructions carefully. He felt every vibration, every bump, and even the tiniest changes in speed and altitude. In just his first hour of flight he had already mastered the 'feel' of the plane.

He studied his gages carefully and absorbed every piece of information he could. Carroll took the controls once again and brought the plane down for a perfect landing.

Over the next few weeks, Jack's classroom time included the fundamental principles of flight, mechanics, meteorology, navigation, communications, and emergency procedures.

Jack and Carroll took another five flights of about two hours each. With each flight, Jack took more and more control of the aircraft. Carroll induced several airborne emergencies on Jack–which he handled according to procedures.

Jack's coordination, physical strength, grace of movement, and excellent judgment of speed and distance placed him among the very top few–two or three–of the scores that Carroll had instructed over the years.

After ten hours of dual instruction, Carroll deemed Jack ready to fly solo.

Jack's eagerness to conduct the flight was evident. Carroll stood on the runway while Jack conducted all of his checks on the ground, then in the cockpit. He returned Jack's 'thumbs-up' to start his engines. After Jack checked all of his gages, he was ready to take off–on his own. He offered Carroll another thumbs-up, which the instructor returned.

Jack pressed the throttle to maximum, raced down the runway, and lifted the plane into the air. He allowed himself just a hint of a smile that he had taken off on his own but he immediately returned to the task at hand. The plane climbed as Carroll watched from the ground. Jack performed all of the tasks Carroll had listed for him–soft banks in each direction followed by more severe turns each way.

Then the most difficult skill–recovering from a stall. Though Jack had successfully practiced the maneuver several times with Carroll by his side, both men knew this would be markedly different as a solo.

Jack dropped his airspeed to a point where the plane began to shake for lack of lift. Just as it began to fall, Jack, true to procedures, pressed the nose forward and dove the plane. As the nose turned down, gravity took over and increased the speed of the plane, allowing more air to pass over its wings, generating more lift. When Jack felt enough speed, and therefore lift, he skillfully pulled the plane out of the dive and back to level flight.

Though Carroll had supreme confidence in Jack's abilities, he allowed himself a huge sigh of relief when Jack leveled out–probably at the exact instant Jack let out his same sigh in the cockpit.

Jack performed a few circles over the airfield, changed altitude by climbing and diving and prepared for his landing.

Carroll took another deep breath—he couldn't help it—it was part of the job—as Jack made his approach.

Jack lined up his approach, dropped his altitude, and touched down right out of the textbook. Carroll had seen few first-time solo landings with such touch.

When the plane came to rest, Carroll hurried over to congratulate Jack.

"That was fantastic! Way to go!" Carroll gushed uncharacteristically.

"Thanks—it was fun!" Jack said as his heart continued to race in response to one of the great adrenalin rushes he had ever experienced."

Robbie and Red Hawk thanked each other for another great trip through time.

DUTY

"Remember that being a citizen is a practice, not a status, and that to do your part will require you to assume responsibility, to embrace and practice the idea of duty, and it will require a measure of personal sacrifice."

Conrad M. Hall

Dear Jim,

Congratulations on your graduation from the United States Naval Academy–what a special accomplishment!

I am certain that the Academy has prepared you well for your future service, but I thought it couldn't hurt to share some thoughts with you based on my sixty-some years, and all of the discussions I had with Jack and all of the letters and diary entries he had concerning military leadership–not to mention my son Bruce who graduated from West Point about nine years ago.

When applicable, I will directly quote Jack's writings or comments. Some of his most poignant thoughts were embedded in much longer letters to my mother, my sisters, or me. Some of his thoughts were directly attributable to others like my father, his teachers and coaches, and fellow officers and airmen. I think a good deal of his thinking, though, was arrived at by the tried and true method–on his own!

Please take these thoughts for what they are worth, and apply your own personality and experience to shape and apply them. (Having been in the 'private sector' for all of these years, I would add that just about all of what Jack observed and thought from his military experience has a civilian corollary and that most of these points hold there, too, though, admittedly, to varying degrees.)

Jack understood the value of teamwork: "We are stationed right in the middle of the area of England where all the American 'heavies' start out to bomb Germany. I happen to be a group operations officer, which causes me to plan and dispatch all of our combat missions. I lead many of these missions as a command pilot, or in other words, I become the pilot that goes along in the lead ship to take care of command decisions en route to and from the target. The training of the various crews have received and their ability to handle successfully situations which may arise are of great importance to me. Beyond this I am concerned about the welfare and spirit of our team.

"A new crew comes to us composed of ten young men excited and eager for battle and scared plenty also. After a few practice missions and lots of advice from the old timers, they are ready for their first 'briefing' and combat mission. They report very early with the other crews to the briefing room and from the excited, scared looks on their faces it's quite easy to pick out the newcomers.

"The briefing starts. The information is released about the target, strength of force, fighter support, and expected enemy opposition. Then all is quiet and the Chaplain is called to have prayers. Many of the crew members present have been trained to be killers, yet at this moment their religion and background come to the front and give them strength, courage, and confidence that can be acquired in no other way."

Here is what Jack said in a letter to me about the inscription on the stick, 'You must first master yourself before you can lead others,' "…I know now, more than ever, what the inscription on our stick meant. I find myself in a constant battle overcoming fear. I think all of us who serve here in any capacity realize the full magnitude of the tasks at hand and know the perils of our missions. To not recognize the danger and accompanying fear would be foolhardy. Yet to be paralyzed by it would be equally foolish. So we have all developed our own methods of pushing our fears out of our minds. We use 'tricks' to stay focused. We know that our work is dangerous–but we also know that we train well and are prepared to execute under difficult conditions. Confidence, preparation, faith in God, and hard work can go a long way in relegating fear to its proper place. Only after we have mastered this technique, can we truly lead our aircrews."

I find this true in the civilian world. Mastering and conquering doubts and fears is a life-long process. Knowledge of self and seeking ways to improve one's self is absolutely critical to success in any field.

Jack had an impeccable sense of <u>duty</u>–one that I am certain you hold, as well. He wrote to my mother "…my duty here is simple. You know that father frequently implored us to 'give more to our country than we take.' Despite all of the time I have spent here and the number of missions I have flown, I still think that I owe my country more of what I can offer. I simply cannot imagine leaving here before the war comes to an end. I will do my best to perform my duty well."

I have found <u>resilience</u> to be a critical trait. This kind of persistent perseverance is a principle by which a select few choose to live. Our country has produced some of the most resilient men: George Washington, Abraham Lincoln, and General Chamberlain, just to name a few. While compromise is sometimes crucial, these men did not settle on deals easily. They stood their ground, and our country has obviously greatly benefited. Learn all that you can, but stand for that in which you believe. It will pay off, trust me. I challenge you to live a life where your reputation is a resilient one.

"…we find ourselves having to bounce back from so many setbacks. I never could have imagined how difficult this task would be. These challenges presented in wartime situations would be difficult–if not impossible–to compare to other challenges I have faced. We must overcome a variety of challenges–mechanical, personnel, tactical, weather–you name it. Yet our men find a way to drive past disappointment and loss to ...."

My own experience mimics Jack's and I agree with him that conditions in war zones cannot be replicated. I would add, though, that 'peacetime' environments–jobs!–frequently produce their own set of vexing problems and issues that require tremendous focus, commitment, courage, and strength.

Finally, Jack and I seem to agree on the tremendous value of a positive attitude. He wrote, "Our men continue to do a remarkable job in the face of many difficulties and stresses. Our group has lost several airplanes and crew in the last two weeks. It is always difficult to receive such news. I do my best to keep the men of our group optimistic and focused on the task at hand. We clearly mourn these losses, but try to dedicate our current and future work to those we have lost along the way. They deserve that much. A way that we attempt to keep positive is by recognizing our grief, addressing it, and working through it together. We will always have each other on whom we can rely, and I have tried to make that clear for my men. I recognize that they have so much work to do and they pay attention to such minute, but important, details that I take some of the extra burden. They need not worry about things that are out of their control. All I ask is that they focus on the current obstacle, attack it wholeheartedly, and come out winning."

I have also realized that there is no need to degrade someone in front of his peers. While we all make mistakes, I encourage you to deal with those situations in a private manner. Team morale and all around respect will go through the roof if you praise individual and team feats in public, but leave the criticisms for meetings behind closed doors. I think your men will respect your leadership and appreciate your advice if you take that approach.

Perhaps the last two lines of Jack's favorite poem will be of some inspiration to you as you engage the daunting tasks

of service and leadership that lie ahead. It is from *Invictus* by
William Ernest Henley (1849–1902):

> I am the master of my fate:
> I am the captain of my soul.

I will, of course, attempt to share more and more of Jack's
thoughts with you as you take to the air in defense of our
country.

My thoughts and prayers go with you.

All my Best,

Doug

LOS ANGELES 1932

"You only lose when you allow yourself to be defeated.
Prepare (practice hard), be disciplined, know your opponent,
and above all, want it!"

Bob Bianchi

U PON Red Hawk's arrival on the next full moon, Robbie had given some thought to his questions.

"Hi, Red Hawk!" Robbie began.

"Hi, Robbie. Is there anything you might want to look at on our trip tonight?"

"Well, I have been thinking about the carvings that Jack did on the stick–the Olympic rings. Do you think we might be able to see some of that part of his story?"

"I think we can do that. But I think we should start that part back in Baltimore. You see, Jack's team at Hopkins had to play a qualifying tournament to represent the United States in the 1932 Olympic Games–very much like the men who played in 1928. Let's go take a look at that part first, O.K.?"

"Great!"

"Well, Robbie, Jack and his Hopkins teammates entered this tournament with the Crescent Lacrosse Club of Brooklyn, NY, the Onondaga Indians, Rutgers University, Syracuse University, St. Johns College of Annapolis, Maryland, Mount Washington, and the University of Maryland. Army had a strong enough team to be considered but ended up

declining the invitation due to military obligations. The format was used to generate some much-needed funds to help the team travel to the Games in California. Hopkins has beaten St. Johns and the Crescents. This is the final against the University of Maryland.

"Maryland is up four to three in the second half. There's Jack." Red Hawk gestured. Having seen him now several times with Red Hawk, Robbie quickly identified Jack. Red Hawk allowed his friend to watch the play from there.

Shortly after Red Hawk and Robbie settled into the scene, Jack received a pass, made a quick dodge to the goal, and got off a shot before the defense could turn him away from the cage, tying the score at four. Maryland then went up by a goal again and Jack made the exact same move with the exact same result, again tying the game–now at five. Jack's linemate, Don Kelly, a brilliant player in his own right who would become a four-time All-American and Hall of Famer, tallied Hopkins' last two goals to secure the hard-fought 7–5 win.

"That looked a little bit like the Poly-Navy game a few years ago when Jack was so good at the end of the game!" Robbie observed.

"I would say so, Robbie. Very similar. I think you are beginning to see that when things are at their toughest out there, Jack somehow seems to make big plays. I think Jack takes his position of responsibility as captain very seriously."

"So that's how Hopkins was chosen to represent the United States," Red Hawk continued as he moved the scene forward a few weeks.

"The team traveled by train across the country and actually missed the opening ceremonies. But they made it here to Los Angeles. The teams from England and Australia were scheduled to be here, too, but had to cancel due to the effects of the world-wide Great Depression. I think Jack and his teammates realize how fortunate they are to have been able to travel here, even during the Depression, and are all very happy to be here.

"So here we are at Olympic Stadium–it is now called the Los Angeles Coliseum–August 7, 1932 as part of the XX Olympiad."

Robbie scanned the crowd–by far the biggest one he had ever seen *or been a part of—over 80,000 people. Most of the people in attendance didn't realize that lacrosse would be played, but they were there to enjoy the men's Marathon Race! These fans must not have known they were one of the biggest audiences before whom these athletes with helmets and sticks, not just running shoes, would perform.*

"The format of the tournament changed when England and Australia announced that they would be unable to participate," Red Hawk shared. "So a three game series was scheduled between Canada and the United States. Since lacrosse here is officially called a demonstration sport, the tournament is being called the World Championship Series.

"I think I should point out one of Jack's teammates that you have heard of. There he is—Pete Reynolds," Red Hawk pointed to the right end of the field. "I'll tell you more about him later—but for now, please watch him during this tournament. I think you will learn a lot by just seeing him play, Robbie."

The boys watched as Jack walked out to the center of the field to take the opening draw on a beautiful, sunny day.

As he arrived at the center mark, Jack happened to look down and found a penny partially exposed in the earth. He bent down to pick it up and noticed the date on it—1910—the year of his birth!

Jack took this as a good omen and slipped the penny into the small crevice in the index finger of his left glove.

Robbie saw this small gesture and wondered what just happened, but as play began, Robbie's attention shifted as he noticed that none of the Canadians were wearing protective headgear and that all of the players were playing both ends of the field and asked Red Hawk about it.

"Why are they all playing the entire field—don't they have an offside rule? And no helmets?"

"No helmets. I guess they feel like they don't need them, Robbie. You may not know this, but helmets were not used until at least 1923 throughout the United States and even then intermittently. And as for the offside rule, the Canadian rules are different. The offside rule was only put into use in the United States not too long ago in 1921," Red

Hawk stated. "So the Hopkins players will have to adjust to the new style."

Robbie noticed the extremely rough play of both teams, particularly in front of each goal where there seemed to be far too many players. He had seen some very rough play in the Poly-Navy plebe and the Mount Washington-Crescent games, but this was at an entirely different level of intensity. Players were knocked to the ground on nearly every loose ball and shot. It seemed that any attacking player who got within ten yards of the goal was gratuitously upended.

The United States trudged through the game to earn a 5–3 victory and a one game to none lead in the series.

Robbie and Red Hawk were quickly taken to a scene two days after this game took place and they watched the two teams play again. It turned out to be another brutal game physically as each team tried to outdo each other's physical challenges. Late in the game, the U.S. scored a goal that was quickly disallowed that would have tied the game.

"Why did they disallow that goal," Robbie begged Red Hawk.

"I don't really know, Robbie. In all my discussions with Jack, he was never able to determine why, either. Canada managed to hold on for a 5–4 win, sending the series to a deciding third game scheduled for August 12th."

The boys watched the game and Robbie was particularly impressed with the USA goalie, Fritz Stude. The Canadian team had to end the game fifteen minutes early to catch a boat back to Vancouver so Hopkins won 7–4 to earn the gold medal.

"Wow! That American goalie was fantastic!" Robbie observed.

"They can be the difference in a game like that, Robbie. I am glad you noticed how well he played."

Red Hawk shared with Robbie that the team enjoyed some social engagements while in Los Angeles and then moved the scene to the train ride back.

Jack sat on the train by himself as he and his teammates had scattered around the coach for more room. Everyone's sore legs were stretched out into the aisles and onto other seats as the boys caught some much-deserved rest. Some read, some tailored their sticks, but most were unresponsive as the motion of the train rocked them into a deep sleep.

Jack had brought Red Hawk's stick with him for the trip and as he sat holding the stick, he pondered the good fortune that had continued to grace his life. He was now twenty-two years old, had spent two years on the Mount Washington club team, just graduated from Johns Hopkins in three years, been named All-State in football at Hopkins and First-Team All-America in lacrosse three times, earned his pilot's license, and just days before, had captained his team to a World Championship at the Olympic Games. He thought of the many people who had helped him. He considered the Olympic championship among the greatest moments of his life. As Jack carefully etched into the stick the Olympic rings, his mind traced back over his life and placed a name and a face with virtually every person who had helped and supported him, beginning, of course, with his family, but quickly including his teachers, coaches, ministers, teammates, and Red Hawk.

Jack thought that this Olympic fame would be short-lived, and the experience would come to an end when he and his teammates stepped off of the train on the east coast, but to top off the incredible journey, the Hopkins contingent was invited to the White House to meet with President Herbert Hoover on September 7th.

"Robbie," Red Hawk began, "I think you know a little about the Turnbull Award—particularly through Captain Lewis—but Pete Reynolds—the player I pointed out the other day is also held in immortality by his teammates."

Robbie quickly interjected, "Right—Coach Scott told us about him. He survived the Bataan Death March only to die on that transport ship?"

"That's right, Robbie. What a tragic story. The '32 team established a Trophy to be awarded annually to a Hopkins lacrosse player to recognize sportsmanship and leadership—the two shining traits of those two *men. It is still awarded today. In fact, for many decades, a player from that team was usually present at the Hopkins awards ceremony to make the presentation."*

"Thanks for the trip, Red Hawk. It was great."

"Glad you enjoyed it. I'll see you soon."

Greatest Possible Gratitude

"Cultivate the habit of being grateful for every good thing that comes to you, and to give thanks continuously. And because all things have contributed to your advancement, you should include all things in your gratitude."

Ralph Waldo Emerson

Dear Robbie,

Enclosed is a copy of a letter that Jack wrote to General Chamberlain's daughter, Daisy Allen, in 1932. There will be more to come. I hope you will enjoy it.

My very best.

Warmly,

Jerri

Robbie opened the enclosed letter.

August 30, 1932

Dear Miss Daisy,

I write to thank you, once again, for your warm and generous support over the past eighteen years and particularly your thoughtful letter and graduation gift. Please forgive my delayed and ungentlemanly response, but shortly after graduation, I began to train with my team to prepare for and then travel to Los Angeles for the Olympic Games, which I will describe shortly.

First–thank you! I am so overwhelmed by your generosity of spirit in sending me the belt buckle worn by your father during the Civil War. I have received no greater gift in my life. I shall wear it proudly and endeavor to conduct myself in a manner of which the general would be proud.

Also, I have already devoured the wonderful book that you sent, your father's memoir, *The Passing of the Armies*, on my trip to Los Angeles.

I am honored and humbled beyond words to have been the recipient of such generous and thoughtful gifts and your continued support.

The last couple of years have been truly amazing for me. In addition to graduating from Johns Hopkins, I earned my pilot certification, and was part of a gold medal-winning lacrosse team that participated in Los Angeles.

I am not sure how much you have heard about the tournament, but I will attempt here to enlighten you to the best of my knowledge. Our team at Johns Hopkins University was chosen to represent the nation in the Olympics. This was such an incredible honor in the first place, and playing in Los Angeles was a great experience. We truly grew as a team and realized how much lacrosse can do for us. We played for everyone on the field, wearing red, white, and blue, but also for all of those who came before us, and for everyone to come after, even long after we are gone. Our games against Canada were emotional and intense, because we have such a great rivalry. I forget all the details. But it was fun!

I know that this country is a magnificent place and I feel privileged to have represented the United States and everyone who is a part of our nation as I wore the red and blue on my lacrosse uniform.

In other news, I am glad to tell you that I have read every book–cover to cover–that you have sent me all these years and

I have them arranged by order of receipt on a special shelf in my library.

I hope you know how much I treasure the relationship that Doug and I have had with your family. Your father's act of kindness to Doug has affected me tremendously–and has changed my life in ways I simply cannot believe.

I know that you are aware of my connection to Red Hawk through this stick. I have enclosed a copy of my diary entries of some of the visits that Red Hawk has provided–particularly those related to your father, Gen. Chamberlain. By my count, it is around twenty! I hope you will enjoy them and I hope they may spark fond memories of him for you.

Enclosed you will also find the participation medal presented to me at the Olympic Games. I send it to you as a token of my gratitude and respect for you, your father, and your family and for all of the kindness and support you have rendered upon me, Doug, and our family all these years.

With the Greatest Possible Gratitude,

Jack

BEAUTIFUL BEYOND DESCRIPTION

"Everyone makes a difference. It's up to each one of us what the difference is."

W. Brooke Tunstall

RED Hawk took Robbie to the Turnbull house in Baltimore about two weeks after Jack returned from his Olympic experience in Berlin, September 9, 1936 and began to describe the scene.

"Robbie, Jack has recently returned from his trip to Berlin and his parents invited the entire family and some special friends for dinner and asked Jack if he could regale the family and guests with details about his experience."

After dinner the family adjourned to their den where Doug, senior introduced Jack.

"We are so glad all of you are here tonight," Doug began. "Thank you for coming. I hope that you know that all of you have meant so much to Jack over the years and he would not be the young man he is today without your support. Each of you has had a special influence on him in your own unique way and have made a difference in his life. Mum and I are so grateful for all you have done for Jack—as well as our other children.

"We asked Jack if he could share some of his experience with all of us and he has kindly agreed. Jack, we are extremely proud of all you have

accomplished—but mostly for the young man you have become. We are very excited to hear about your travels."

Jack stood in front of the guests and began modestly, "Well, dad has just said what I would have said—thank you to all of you for your support. I hope that I will be able to repay you at some point in the future. For now, I think all I can do is take the goodness you have rendered upon me and try to pass it along as best I can. Thank you.

"Well, as far as my trip goes—wow! I kept a detailed diary of my travels beginning at the end of July and going through the end of the trip around August 25. If you don't mind, I have reviewed the diary, highlighted some of the events, and can embellish upon them. We'll save time at the end for questions," Jack closed with a smile.

"Most of you have heard me speak about my experience in Los Angeles. This one could not have been more different—in just about every way. Overall, I had a wonderful experience—but everything about this event was so much more serious and generally lacked the incredible amount of fun we had in L.A.

"I can probably start with the composition of our field hockey team. We were all selected through a tryout, so few of our players had any friendships or experience playing together. In L.A. we were all teammates from Hopkins and entered the tournament with an incredible bond.

"All of the guys worked hard to get our team to gel—but it was just much more difficult. And as a country, we are not particularly strong in field hockey—so we struggled in most of our games. It was still a truly great honor to be a part of the United States team.

"Another difference was the way we traveled. In going to L.A., we took a train all the way and had a great time. This time we were on an ocean liner and, since I didn't know my teammates very well, I spent a good amount of time sunning on the deck and doing some exercise. I read quite a bit—including The Epic of America.

"Believe it or not—the one thing that probably disappointed me the most was the poor mail service! Since I had quite a bit more down time than I am used to, I was hoping the mail would come more regularly—but *it didn't. And some of the mail had been opened by German officials and resealed!*

"I guess the biggest difference was Germany itself. We stayed in a nice Olympic village about fifteen miles from Berlin–and we had just about everything we needed right there in the village. I traveled to Berlin a number of times to watch other events–mostly swimming. There were uniformed soldiers all over the place rendering the Nazi salute. They were all very stoic. They had a military band playing the entire time from nine in the morning until five at night–which began to wear on us after a while. The country itself was beautiful–but things were much, much more relaxed and fun in Los Angeles.

"I'd love to say that the field hockey was the best part–like the actual lacrosse was in L.A., but the best part for me was the travel and the places we visited which I will discuss in a little bit.

"I have a couple of passages from my diary that I would like to read directly. This was from our trip over:

'About seven o'clock we got to the tip of England–called 'Land's End' and from there on we were in the English Channel and had the interesting shoreline to watch. Every little while we could see a castle perched up on the high banks and always those rolling green hills with a row of trees dividing the fields now and then. I think of all the European countries or at least the ones on this side, I would rather tour the British Isles than any. We passed many little fishing boats and freight steamers. About four o'clock we got to Plymouth and that really is a beautiful little city. There are three forts guarding the harbor and a castle on the point. We couldn't go into the harbor but we could see plenty from where we were. The towns of England seem so planned in their layout and they are immaculate. Everything is so clean.

"Just before leaving, a Spanish galleon sailed by. It looked just like a pirate ship and even had the guns out the side. I later found out it was an exact duplicate of Sir Francis Drake's flagship, the Golden Hind, *and that it was sailed twice a year to keep the seams tight.*

We were lucky to be there at the time. What an opportunity, that we were able to see it.

'August 2. After lunch, we went to the stadium to see the first races. The stadium was jammed in spite of the threatening rain. Jesse Owens broke the world record for the 100 meter and looked like he was coasting.... The fuehrer was there and shook hands with all the winners ...Got home late from the stadium and just finished supper. That moon looks awful swell, all round, coming up through those trees. Guess I better get to bed before I start wondering where all those letters are that haven't come.

'August 4. Went back to the stadium and saw more records broken. Jesse Owens has broken the world record in every event he has been in. He is an incredible athlete! I hope to have the honor of meeting him while we are here, representing the same country.

'Jesse Owens is great. I have yet to meet him, but watching him from the stands is so incredible. He runs with such ease! I wish I could do that. He is so graceful, but swift. He makes his competitors look like they are running through water, but not a muscle is tense on his face. He is truly a spectacle.

'August 12. Went to Potsdam the other day and I kicked myself for not studying more history. The other fellows knew all the stories connected to Frederick the Great and the castle at San Soucci, etc. but I couldn't remember it and could only appreciate it from the artistic view. We went on a little river steamer and although the weather was bad as usual, the trip was beautiful. The banks are completely utilized with castles and homes. All beautifully taken care of and planted with silver birch and weeping willow. It is an impressive sight in Germany to see the way land is so completely used. There are no tall buildings but every piece of land, no matter how small, is being lived on. There are thousands of little shacks that have only a room but are as neat as can be and immaculate. Along the river the lots were bigger, maybe an acre or two, but every inch of the

ground beautifully taken care of. Potsdam is a beautiful old city and the gardens of San Soucci are beautiful beyond description. We went through all the palaces and gardens and must have walked ten miles. The buildings are beautiful, but the gardens are the most beautiful part in my estimation.

'Heard the Berlin Philharmonic last night here at the village and it was marvelous. They played in the birch cluster at the foot of the hill and were lit by torch light. The setting was perfect and I have never been more thrilled by music. Afterwards the fireworks they had were unbelievable. They far overshadowed the fireworks of the first night and they were the best I have ever seen. I can't describe them but they were wonderful.'

"I think that my overall experience was as compelling as Los Angeles. I was so proud to represent my country. The excitement and pride that I experienced in winning the gold medal in L.A. equaled my frustration in not doing as well this time in field hockey.

"The difficulty I had in communicating with all of you back home was extremely frustrating. But it also helped me realize all the more how much my family and friends mean to me. I think I learned to become more patient on this trip. I really didn't have a choice.

"I don't think there is any way to replicate the cultural experience of seeing the sights of such rich history and beauty. I experienced art, architecture, music, and other aesthetics on a scale that I didn't know existed and for that alone I am glad of this trip. At the same time, I began to see the whole world coming together as one, and how incredible that really is. However, I saw hatred at the same time, between countries and between people and I did not like seeing that.

"I'll never be able to thank you all enough for your support—though it didn't come in a timely fashion due to the mail," Jack paused and smiled, "it means much more to me than you probably think. Thank you."

Red Hawk and Robbie waved goodbye to each other for another month.

NEXT GROUNDER

"Coaching is all about relationships. It doesn't happen on chalk-boards, with titles, or in newspaper articles. Transformational coaching occurs only when people believe in you and choose to follow you because they know that you believe in them, too."

Joe Erhmann
InSideOut Coaching

Robbie,

I hope all is well. Here is another good letter from my father to me. Hope you enjoy.

My best to you and your family.

"Respect the Game!"
Bruce

Robbie read the letter.

August 30, 1948
Dear Bruce,

I was fortunate to have played lacrosse (and football) with some really great players and coaches. My coach at Johns Hopkins, "Father Bill" Schmeisser, was certainly one of the major influences upon my life. He is the namesake of the Award that recognizes the most outstanding defensive player in the country. Tyler Campbell of Princeton University, a Gilman graduate, was the first recipient in 1942 and, as you know, perished in the service of our country.

As you begin your junior year, let me beg you to become the type of person and leader we would hope for—like Tyler and Coach Schmeisser.

Coach Schmeisser used to have a little mantra he called, 'Next Grounder.' Simply put, it means to focus on the task at hand. As it applies to lacrosse, of course, the ground ball or, as he called them, grounders, were (and still are) the most critical element of the game. But the phrase is symbolic of every aspect of the game—grounders, passes, shots, dodges, rides, faceoffs, saves, defensive stops—everything. So, 'Next Grounder' could really mean 'Next Play' or the next few seconds in any particular situation.

As you grow into more and more challenging and important leadership roles, I would ask you to think about the value of constantly focusing your thoughts and energies forward and specifically to the immediate task at hand.

You will obviously benefit from retrospective analysis on certain aspects of your performance. You will also benefit from designing and developing long-range plans and goals. But the overwhelming majority of your focus should be on what is coming just ahead. I have seen so, so many people become crippled by negative thoughts of events and experiences that have long since passed. Others have become frozen by the dread of what is going to happen tomorrow. I have tried hard to teach myself to focus on what is happening now and in the very short future.

In a lacrosse game, you certainly want to think about the outcome of an entire game. But I think great teams and great players win each individual play over and over again. They are able to exercise and execute great fundamentals under pressure and when they are fatigued. I've always thought that if your team leads by, let's say, five goals at any point in the game there can be a natural tendency to let down some and lose your edge. Conversely, if your team trails by those same five goals, you may become dejected or try to do too much to recover. In either case, the best course of action is to play as if the score is tied—or zero-zero, as our coach used to say—in order to apply the appropriate attention to each little play that, added together, turn into big plays for your team.

My coaches would frequently remind us that the same tactics were applicable in all phases of their lives. Break big challenges (winning games) into small parts and working hard to conquer each one. Athletics, academics, business (Coach Schmeisser was an attorney and a *volunteer* coach), marriage–all of them.

I think one of the great accomplishments known to history was that of the 'Corps of Discovery,' better known to most people as the Lewis and Clark Expedition. (I won't get into the debate of what the exploration of the West meant in terms of displacing Native Americans, etc.–it certainly could be argued that it had a direct and detrimental effect on those peoples.) Based only on the sheer difficulty of what the Corps accomplished–a trip from St. Louis to the Pacific Ocean and back with only the provisions they could carry on their specially designed 'keelboat' to help navigate up the Missouri River and their own skills, strength, patience, and moxie–is truly amazing–at least to me. In the journal kept by Army Captain William Clark–the co-leader–he frequently wrote simply, "Continue on." I think that the pragmatic and iron-willed Clark balanced the somewhat melancholy and perhaps more brilliant Captain Meriwether Lewis. It seems that Clark knew that the Corps was tasked to move through unknown and uncharted territory for about two years by simply taking on the monumental task one day–perhaps one mile or even *one step*–at a time.

Or how about the old adage that goes something like, 'A journey of a thousand miles begins with one step'? I would add that that journey also includes many, many more steps almost none of which is any more or any less important than any other.

So this year, I would ask you to work on teaching yourself to break each challenge you encounter into its fundamental smaller parts and go about attacking each one with focus and determination. I think you'll be very pleased with the results.

Be a leader. It is not going to be easy—but you have your mother's and my faith that you will rise to every challenge you face this year.

Next Grounder!

With Love and Pride,
Dad

THE PENNY

"Everyone needs to realize that they set an example for someone. It is so very important to be the best example you can be. The lives of young people can be changed forever by seeing people do what is right."

Stanley Tyron
WW II Prisoner of War
Prisoners of Hope

O N the next full moon, Red Hawk and Robbie went to see Jack at the Mount Washington Lacrosse Club in Baltimore, Maryland. May 1937.

"Robbie," Red Hawk began, "we are back at Mount Washington. A few months ago we were here watching Jack and Doug play when Jack was still at Poly. Now it is just Jack.

"This is just a practice, but I thought you should see this. The Mount Washington team just finished practice a few minutes ago. Most of the guys have gone home but Jack and Oster 'Kid' Norris—remember him from the game of ten years ago?—are still here throwing around with their ball boy, Brooke Tunstall. At this point in time, Brooke is a ninth grader at Poly, which isn't far from here. He rides his bike to all of the Mount practices after he finishes his practice or game at school. He just shags balls for these guys but sometimes the old guys will stay and throw or shoot with him for a while. Let's just watch for a little bit from here."

Robbie watched as the two Mt. Washington stars threw in a triangle, changing hands and skills, with young Brooke for about fifteen minutes. Then they had Brooke cut to the cage and fed him passes. Brooke absorbed every second he was with Jack and 'Kid.' After about one hundred shots from both sides of the goal, Jack had Brooke dodge against him while he played dummy defense on him. After a few dodges, Jack offered some pointers to the boy and then asked Norris to play defense for a few sets.

"Here, Brooke, keep your stick tight to your head when you go through that dodge," Jack counseled as he tipped Brooke's stick closer to his head.

Jack then helped Brooke with his defensive—or riding—skills. "Brooke, a lot of people forget how important riding is in lacrosse. I can tell you that every one of my coaches worked with us really hard on this and it always paid off. Let's go through a little of that, O.K.?"

Without even verbally responding, Brooke took his defensive position on Jack who carried the ball at half speed as if he were attempting to run past the youngster.

Jack continued, "So here is the critical point, Brooke. Make sure that you get the proper angle to what our coaches call the 'front' side. Most players will try to fake you at this point. Don't buy it. Just keep working to stay on the front and you'll be amazed at how effective this is. You'll need to display some strength, toughness, and persistence, but your team will benefit a lot. Here try to turn me as the ball carrier."

Jack jogged slowly with the ball to give Brooke a target. As Brooke improved his angle and strength, Jack moved a little faster and with more strength each time. Brooke made the appropriate adjustments. Then 'Kid' offered himself as the target for a few sets while Jack inspected Brooke's technique.

"Great, Brooke. Great! You are doing it right. There is always room for improvement, but that is great. I'm telling you—this is a game-changer!" Jack crowed.

'Kid' and Jack worked through some groundball drills with young Brooke as well, demonstrating proper technique and offering critiques as the youngster worked on his skills.

"We can't say enough about ground balls, either, Brooke," 'Kid'
offered as he demonstrated.

"You have to work hard to get all the way down on the ball. If you
don't get your whole body through the scoop–you'll be checked and lose
the ball again. So drive your hips and entire body through the ball–don't
reach for it or rake it backwards. That won't work against good players
or good teams. The real key is to make sure you get the ball on the first
try–our coaches in the old days used to call them 'first-time grounders.'
It's really important!"

The whole lesson took about an hour and it was now almost dark as
Robbie and Red Hawk watched.

Red Hawk shared, "Robbie, Jack and 'Kid' worked with Brooke
a lot in this fashion. Just staying after practice for a while and helping
him with his fundamental skills. There is one more part I would like for
you to see."

Red Hawk moved the scene to a similar night a few weeks later. After
another set of drills that Jack and 'Kid' helped Brooke with, Jack took off
his lacrosse gloves and pulled his lucky penny from the crease in the left
index finger and handed it to Brooke.

"Brooke, I found this penny on the field of Olympic Stadium when I
walked out for the first faceoff of the 1932 Olympics. I have always considered it took be good luck for me. I have carried it with me everywhere
I have gone. See how it slips in and out of the glove pretty easily here,"
Jack demonstrated. "I keep it in my pocket all the time. I took it with
me to Berlin for the 1936 Olympics. I think I have gotten quite a bit of
good luck from it these last few years. I'd like you to have it."

Brooke stood quietly and wasn't sure how to react.

"Here, try to slide it into your glove. It should go in like on mine.
It'll stay in there while you play and you can take it out easily, too," Jack
offered.

"Thanks, Jack," Brooke said gratefully. He could only gather the
response, "I hope it brings me the same kind of luck it has brought you.
I'll do my best to take care of it."

Robbie continued to gaze on in amazement of what he had witnessed—yet another incredible gesture that he had witnessed courtesy of Red Hawk and these magical journeys.

"I think it would be impossible to overstate what Jack meant to Brooke all those years. He was a perfect role model for Brooke. Jack tracked Brooke's progress throughout his career and offered him support and encouragement all the way. Jack told me frequently that he felt an obligation to pass on all of the support that he had been given by his teammates—particularly 'Kid' and the others from Mount Washington. Brooke was lucky to be one of those beneficiaries.

"I'd like for you to see one more piece of Brooke's story, Robbie," Red Hawk said as he shifted scenes in their time travel.

The boys were now at Homewood Field at Johns Hopkins during halftime of a game in 1977.

As the scene began, Robbie immediately noted that the event taking place on the field looked exactly like the one Red Hawk had taken him to see Captain Lewis' Hall of Fame induction ceremony—and the person about to speak looked like Doug! Robbie looked at Red Hawk, "Is that Doug?"

"Yes, Robbie, he had the honor of presenting Brooke for induction into the Hall of Fame! I guess you could include this in the 'Circle of Life' category."

Robbie and Red Hawk listened as Doug began.

"Ladies and gentlemen, I am Douglas Turnbull, junior, and I have the honor and pleasure of inducting W. Brooke Tunstall into the National Lacrosse Hall of Fame. Most of you remember Brooke's brilliant playing career here at Hopkins in 1947 and 1948. He played the game with great spirit, talent, and reverence. If you every saw Brooke play, you would be inclined, I think, to compare him to an orchestra conductor, bringing out the skill and beauty in all of his teammates. He was a joy to watch. He may have also had one of the more interesting careers of anyone I know.

"You may not know this, but Brooke went to Union because he

was offered financial help for his participation in lacrosse and football. Brooke was a member of the North team in the Annual North-South All-Star Game in 1942 while a freshman. Then while playing football at Union, he suffered a complex broken leg—they said he may not ever play sports again. They didn't know Brooke, did they?

"When World War II began, Brooke knew he wanted to serve as a Marine. While waiting for an opening at Boot Camp, Brooke attended a Marine pre-training unit at Cornell University. It just happened to be during the spring, and the Cornell Lacrosse team was delighted to have him! He was chosen as an All-American in the 1944 season.

"From there, Brooke completed Marine Corps Boot Camp at Paris Island, South Carolina, and then Officer Training at Quantico, Virginia. He then shipped to Hawaii to prepare for the Invasion of Japan. Fortunately for all of us, and particularly Brooke, the war ended after the dropping of the atomic bombs in Japan. So Brooke and his comrades were spared the likelihood of Invasion. Brooke left the Marine Corps as a First Lieutenant and, much to our delight, enrolled at Johns Hopkins, where he was became a two-time First-Team All-American, two-time national champion, participated in the North-South Game twice, and was a two-time recipient of the Jack Turnbull Award, named in memory of my late brother.

"Brooke, therefore, is probably the only player in the history of lacrosse to play in the North-South Game three times, while playing for both teams!

"Brooke has enjoyed a successful career in the business world in New Jersey with his wife, Peg, and their three daughters. It gives me the greatest possible pride and personal joy to present W. Brooke Tunstall for induction into the National Lacrosse Hall of Fame. Brooke,"

Brooke beamed as he approached Doug to receive his Hall of Fame plaque.

"Thank you, Doug. This is nothing less than a boyhood dream come true for me. I can't thank the Hall of Fame Committee, you, or your family enough for all of your support for what has been, in effect, my whole life. You know that none of my modest success on the field would

have been possible without you, Jack, Kid Norris, my teammates and coaches at Union, Cornell, and Hopkins.

"*Ladies and gentlemen, I must tell you that the only reason that I stand before you today, is because of the goodness that was directed toward me by countless people. But Jack Turnbull was the most influential person in my life. He was my idol and I think of him every day, hoping that I can be a fraction of the person he was. I very much share this honor with Jack and many others. Thank you all.*"

"*I hope you enjoyed that trip, Robbie,*" Red Hawk closed.

"*Wow! Great. Thanks. See you soon.*"

THE GREATEST ASSET THAT I POSSESS

Be Strong. Be Accountable. Never Complain.
motto of LT (SEAL) Brendan Looney, USN

Robbie,

I hope all is well. I have enclosed several letters from Jack to his mother in 1944. I thought you might like to try to get a sense of some of his more routine concerns but there are a number of very compelling observations scattered throughout (at least in my mind). I hope you'll be as struck as I have been by Jack's sense of gratitude to his mother and family.

Not all of these are dated–so we did our best to try to arrange them in what seemed to be the proper sequence. The woman, May, of whom Jack frequently refers is his mother's sister, who moved in with them after her husband passed some years earlier. Jerri wanted me to include the last letter that Jack wrote to his sister Anne–it has always been her favorite. She considers it the most beautiful letter and a true testament to what a little sister means to an older brother. Enjoy.

Best,
Bruce

[Sunday in March 1944]

Dear Mother,

It has been a long time and a busy one. We have just finished our final inspection and we passed with the highest mark of any unit that has ever gone overseas. That makes the hard work seem worthwhile. We have really been at it the past few weeks and now sending everyone we can on final leave. That makes our work now doubly tough because it makes us shorthanded for the packing. It looks as if we will go out on schedule, which leaves us very little time to do a million details. I tried to call you all on the telephone today but they were announcing a four hour delay and I couldn't wait that long. Our new aircraft are coming in awful fast now and they are really beautiful. No paint and just as shiny as a new bicycle. They are really equipped to do the job that I know we can and will do very shortly.

Our unit is really starting to be a good one and we are looking forward to one good feature of war. That is the good fellowship, self-sacrifice, and teamwork that comes from fighting for a common goal. I'm confident that we are well on the way now and that this year should nearly finish up the European Theatre. Anyhow, I pray so.

I'm on my way to El Paso tomorrow for a much needed day off and a little visit to Mexico. Then back to packing and finishing the training that we are all eager to have now that the time is near.

Give my best to all the folks and say hello to "Mac" and "Dan" for me. Tell Anne not to worry about Marsh, that the <u>Army</u> will take care of him.

Sure glad to hear of Henry's back. He will make a good officer.

All my love,
Jack

Friday

Dear Mother,

It was swell talking to you and Anne today. It only took about thirty seconds to get you, which was a pleasant surprise. I have just finished packing and loading my airplane and we are all set. I'll send you my APO # as soon as I learn what it is.

I have sold my car at a profit and sent the check to the bank for deposit. I am canceling the insurance on it and asking them to send the check to you. Starting May 1st you will receive $300 per month and I'll receive the remainder overseas. Each time a bank statement comes let me know what the total is and I'll keep my checkbook straight that way. I'll probably not write any checks overseas but instead will send money orders home. I would like to keep my bank balance above two thousand dollars so feel perfectly free to use all the money you need for anything you need. If I start getting too big a balance once in a while either buy me a savings bond or send some to Choice to invest for me. (Also a few presents for my god-children.)

I'm sending a lot of clothes home that I won't need. The wool clothing you can give away. The cotton you better save for me. Also in the box will be an envelope with lots of different things in it. Feel perfectly free to go through it at will.

I am really eager to go now as I know we are well trained and have the best equipment we can get. Therefore, the quicker I go the sooner I return. I am taking along a little prayer book and expecting to use it, but the greatest asset that I possess is the body you gave me and the training and upbringing that you have instilled in me. I feel perfectly confident that with this and the good Lord's help I'll never meet a situation that I won't be able to cope with successfully. I'll never stop being grateful to you for the love and care you have given me.

I'll write, probably, more often now that all the training is behind me and it won't be long before this awful mess is behind us.

Take care of yourself and don't try to do too much. Be good

to yourself. You are due a nice rest. I wish you could go to
Florida with Anne.

All my love,
Jack

Sunday [March]

Dear Mother,

I just finished your nice letter and I'm glad to hear that
spring at last seems to have arrived. The picture of Anne is good
but Mac seems to be making faces. I guess Marshall thinks he is
beautiful even though he looks a little like himself. The sleeping
bag arrived O.K. and I'll soon be shipping my excess equipment
home. They won't let me take my lacrosse stick or my bicycle
so I'll ship the first and sell the latter. I've been offered $1000
for it but I think I'll get $1100 tomorrow. We have just about
completed our training and are only flying the new aircraft to
put a little time on them before the big trip. We gave the whole
outfit two days off (today and tomorrow) but as usual, I have
had to work. I am starting to get sunburned and we'll be leaving
just at the right time before it gets too hot. I'll call you before I
go and I guess the best place will be at Anne's. The lines are so
jammed that it will probably have to be a morning call.

The way things look now we will probably be back in a matter
of months. They are making so many raids that we will probably
finish our 25–50 raids in a couple of months. I sure hope so.

I have sent Anne a pair of stockings but they say you can't tell
whether they are any good or not so I only bought one pair for her.

We are going to have a big party to wind things up on Tuesday
night so from then on packing, etc. will really keep me hopping.
I'll write at least once more and will give you a call before we leave.

We feel pretty proud being the only group that has been
really ahead of time. We really have a swell outfit and I am
sure they will really take care of themselves when the going gets

tough. I wish I could fly with them every mission but I'm afraid the old desk weighs too heavy on me in the job that I have.

I'm sending you a book by Lin Yutang that really hits the bull on the nose. I sure wish there were more men like him to sit on the peace tables.

I'll write soon again.

All my love,

Jack

Friday [Postmarked 1 APR 1944, New Mexico]

Dear Mother,

I have no idea how long it's been since I have written you because I'm so busy I hardly know the day of the week. Yesterday and today, we had the Army Air Force inspectors, the 2nd Air Force inspectors, the 16th Wing inspectors, and the Air Base inspectors all here at once. After forgetting we existed for all this time they all wake up at once and realize we are due to go very shortly now. So they all flock around and rush! rush! rush!

Spring has really arrived here now. The temp. is up to about eighty in the daytime but it still freezes nearly every night. I sure wish you and May could come out here for a few weeks. The sun would really do you lots of good. However unless you would fly the trip would be terrible.

I got a letter from Henry and I sure am glad to hear he got a commission. He would have more fun as a "gob" but he will be more useful as a leader.

Also got a letter from Fritzc and he tells me he is the father of a 7 lb. 11 oz. son. He is something. Just mentioned it casually as if it was nothing.

I hope to get to El Paso Monday and do a little shopping, also get a price on my car so I'll be able to sell it when I leave. I have gotten a box together to ship all my loose ends in when I leave. I'll screw the lid on and send you the papers on it.

I flew today on a Wing formation, which is a combination of two groups. There are seventy planes to a group so you can see we had quite a formation. I led it and the general was quite pleased. We have a swell outfit here and I will be awful glad to get out of all this mess of training into a nice quiet war.

Well, give my best to all you see and take care of yourselves. Tell May if I thought it possible to ship it, I would sure ruin one of her chocolate cakes. However, I'm afraid the mails would ruin it. A boy received a box of honey and jam the other day and the bottles were broken. You should have seen the mess. I'll write again soon.

Lots of love,
Jack

Wednesday, April
Herington Army Air Field Herington, Kansas

Dear Folks:

This is sure a cold place after Alamogordo. The wind just sweeps across these plains and really cuts right through you. I can't tell you where or when we leave here but I do hope to give you another call on the phone before we go.

Things are going swell and I feel much relieved now that our training is behind us.

I have shipped home a box of excess things. Do what you want with them except for the envelope with all my papers. Keep that somewhere that will be safe.

I'll drop you a line every chance I get.

All my love,
Jack

April 11, 1944

Dear Mother:

Golly it is hot! This part of the world is really something. We have been awful lucky so far with the weather and happy to have the best until we complete our travel.

The world really gets big when you start moving around

it. I feel like I am a million miles from home and as far as any similarity goes I guess I am. No troubles whatsoever so far and we are hoping things continue this way. I still don't know my APO # although I do know my destination. I'll send it to you as I know definitely what it is.

Take it easy and I'll write soon. I spent Easter all day in the air.

All my love,

Jack

April 14, 1944

Dear Mother:

Well, here I am in Africa and it is really some place. The weather is beautiful and I've run into lots of my friends. This is really an interesting city and fairly modern. The Arabs are an interesting people but the sanitation is really something. You see the donkeys and men all standing in the gutter drinking the same dirty water. There are thousands of beggars and also thousands of Jews that have left Europe. Our mess and quarters are served and cleaned by Italian prisoners that seem pretty happy with their work. The mountains in the distance are very lovely and it brings back the old geography to me to make me realize that there are mountains in Africa. I've sort of thought of Africa as jungles and desert only.

We are all well and anxious to get the war over soon and if I have anything to do with it, we'll be home soon. I lost the lacrosse ball you sent me so if you can get me another and please send it to me at the above address. It sure is remarkable how quick the supply situation changes. A few days' flight and it really makes you appreciate the plenty you have back in the U. S. Well, the first chance I get I'll write you again. There is quite a difference writing a letter when you have to think all the time of what you can't say. Give my best to all the gang and the family and I'll see you as soon as I can.

All my love,

Jack

June 2, 1944

Dear Mother:

Just a short one to let you know how lucky I am. I've just been promoted again and realize more as the time goes on that everything I accomplished, with seemingly not too much effort, is because of what you and father have done for us kids. When I take time to think about things, I become pretty restless to get rid of this war and turmoil and settle down to the real job of my life which is to raise a family along the same lines that you have shown us. If I can get started and do the job you two have done I'll sure be satisfied.

I'm enclosing a snap, which I think is very flattering but most people think is good. I like it anyhow. We are still progressing pretty rapidly in getting set up but we are not near the perfection that I want. We have one great trouble, in that the crews make only thirty combat missions and then are replaced. That means we have a continual training program to train new crews for combat. You feel as if you never catch up.

You remember Jack who lived over Charley on the Blvd. He was killed when that transport ship was sunk in the Mediterranean. Another flyer killed by other than aviation. I sure feel sorry for Dottie.

As I wrote you last night and there is little I can tell you, I will close here.

It sure sounds funny to be called "Colonel." I'll try to write more often in the future.

All my love,
Jack

October 14, 1944

My Dear Sister,

I hope that you are well. Thank you for your recent letters and goodies. I share them with the men—so you are becoming rather famous here in our group. So many of our airmen are rather young—eighteen to twenty-three or so. I must remind them constantly that you are married!

Things here are about the same. We have flown five missions since I last wrote. Each mission is an incredible challenge to complete successfully—but our men continue to rise to every occasion.

There are constant reminders of how precarious our situation is over here. Our barracks are frequently missing many men from the previous day, as they simply do not return from their flights. Some crash, some are shot down, some are lost with no trace, some may have had to divert to neutral countries such as Switzerland due to mechanical difficulties. In any case, our emptying barracks tell the story of loss on a daily basis.

I think every boy should be blessed with a sister—not to mention three of them—like Doug and I have! If I had a magic wand to wave to make some sort of miracle happen, I would wave it first, I guess, to end this terrible war. Right after that, though, I would wave it to allow you to see yourself as I see you. Your wit, intelligence, talent, and grace exceed my ability to convey what they look like to me other than to say that I am the luckiest brother in the world. Your love and support have meant everything to me over here.

I will do my best to get myself and my men home safely. Please give my love to Mum, May, Helen, Libby, and Doug.

Back to work.

Much love, Anne,

Jack

Fly to Honor

"Dedicate your own work ... to someone you admire
or matters in your life. You can infuse your work
with purpose and meaning when you think of it as a gift."
Daniel Pink,
A Whole New Mind

A S Robbie fell into sleep on the next full moon, Red Hawk
visited him and the boys went to the ready room of the 44th
Bomb Group. Shipdam, England on 27 AUG 1944.

Group Operations Officer Lt. Col. Turnbull was completing his pre-
flight briefing for the group's mission of thirty-four bombers and two
radar planes to an aero-engine factory in Basdorf, Germany. After Jack
concluded his remarks and the chaplain offered a prayer, Jack continued
in uncharacteristic fashion, "Gentlemen, I would like to share with you
a gesture of which I have become aware. Technical Sergeant D'Andrea
shared with me recently that he has carried a flag of the United States
on each of his missions while here—and wrapped the flag around a note
of dedication to someone who has been important in his life. He plans to
present these flags to these good people upon his return to the states as a
'Thank You' for all of the support they have provided him.

"I must tell you how moved I was to hear of this and would ask
each of you to consider enacting a similar gesture. I plan to. Not that
any of us need any particular extra incentive to do our very best in a
war zone—ending this terrible war and returning safely to our families

should be motivation enough. But, like Sergeant D'Andrea, perhaps you could think of this gesture as a way to thank someone who has helped you. I am certain they would be moved beyond words to receive such a tribute. This is such a thoughtful, generous, and brilliant gesture that I wish I had thought of it myself!" Turnbull shared with a rare smile.

Red Hawk then moved the scene forward to 24 OCT 1944–six days after Jack's final mission.

    Flight surgeon Colonel Drew Finn arrived at the convent in Petegem-aan-de-Leie/Deinze, Belgium to conduct an investigation into the accident that cost thirteen American lives. The nuns conveyed their sorrow to Finn and recounted to the investigating officer all of the difficult details related to the actual crash of October 18, and the disposition of the bodies.

    "Twelve airmen perished in the crash, but Colonel Turnbull was alive until around noon the next day," Sister Christine reported.

    The nuns invited Colonel Finn to sit, and presented him with the flag they had recovered from Jack's flight suit, having returned the contents to their original form.

    "Please open the flag, colonel," Sister Lutgarde asked.

    Finn hesitated and then delicately untied the ribbons and placed them on a nearby table. The nuns nodded for Finn to continue. As he gently unwrapped the flag, Finn noticed the two pieces of paper inside. The first paper read:

"Fly to Honor"

I carry this flag of the United States with me–close to my heart–on this mission in Honor of someone who has helped and supported me during my life. I want each of these people to know what they have meant to me and, more importantly, that the goodness they have rendered upon me has inspired me to share that kindness with the airmen under my command and, I'd like to think, make me a better officer.

I am deeply honored and humbled to wrap these precious contents in red, white, and blue ribbons that were sent to me by my younger sister, Anne, in securing a number of packages she sent to me.

Should I not return safely from this flight, I would ask the appropriate parties to deliver this flag and note as well as the other flags and notes of dedication, gratitude, and thanks from previous successful missions located in my footlocker at my base, to be returned to my brother, Douglas C. Turnbull, Jr. of Baltimore, Maryland, for appropriate disposition.

Colonel Finn glanced at the nuns, whose eyes indicated that he should continue reading the second sheet, which read:

"I Fly Group Mission #84 on 18 OCT 1944 to Honor"

My high school lacrosse coach and math teacher, Mr. D.A. Melosh who recognized and supported my talents and interests and helped me push through an admitted lack of enthusiasm in my academic affairs and helped me become the player, student, and officer that I am today. Thank you, Coach!

Colonel Finn slowly slid deeper into the chair, his eyes staring vacantly ahead with his mind stuck between being overwhelmed by such a gesture and the practical reality of determining a proper course of action.

"Among Colonel Turnbull's final words were 'There are more. Please find. Please send,'" Sister Lutgarde offered softly to the flight surgeon, shaking him from his trance. "Then he thanked us."

"There are more?"

"We found these other twelve flags on the fallen airmen."

"So all of the crewmen had one of these?" Finn asked.

"Yes, sir. Here in this box—all properly labeled. We asked permission to take them from all of the victims to ensure safe keeping for all of them."

"I have never heard of this before. Carrying an American flag on a combat mission to honor someone? Seems like we should be honoring them," Finn responded, more to himself than to the nuns.

Finn carefully pulled each of the airman's flags from the box and read their dedications while the nuns sat quietly. He paused for several minutes to process what he was experiencing. He flipped back to the first sheet of Jack's notes and reread the part that said he had more of these in his footlocker.

Finn continued to whisper to himself, *"So Colonel Turnbull has more of his own back at his base. It says on each of these from the other airmen that they have a similar collection in their footlockers, as well. This is absolutely incredible."*

He addressed the nuns, *"Sisters, on behalf of the United States, please accept my sincerest thanks for all you have done for these airmen and our country. I wish that this situation had not intruded into your lives as it has and that it would have had a more pleasant ending. I thank you for your care and attention in particular to Colonel Turnbull's fight for life. I will share your efforts with my superior officers and his family if I am fortunate enough to have the chance. May God continue to bless you and help move this terrible war to a speedy end."*

After completing his investigation and arriving back at Shipdam, Finn found the notes for each aviator in their footlockers and pored over each one. He pondered the monumental task at hand—thirteen airmen's personal belongings to prepare for return to their families, thirteen letters to grieving families, scores of "Fly to Honor" dedications, and, with some remarkably good luck, a visit to the Turnbull family in Baltimore at some point after the conclusion of the war.

Red Hawk turned Robbie's attention to the work Finn performed on Jack's case.

Finn slowly flipped through Jack's dedications again and attempted to visualize the reaction the recipients might have when they became aware of Jack's gesture of gratitude to them. Finn read them:

Mission #64 30 SEP 1944 to my mother, Elizabeth Turnbull and my late father, Douglas C. Turnbull, Sr. Words here cannot convey the support they have provided me in every respect.

Mission #67 2 OCT 1944 to my sisters Helen, Libby, and Anne, and my brother Doug. I am the luckiest brother in the world to have these four people as my siblings (one flag for each).

Mission #75 7 OCT 1944 to my mentor, teammate, and coach Oster 'Kid' Norris. All of the time we shared together, all the experiences, all of the advice. I cannot express my gratitude enough.

Mission #80 11 OCT 1944 to My flight instructor Jack Carroll, a fellow Hopkins alumnus and Phi Kappa Psi fraternity brother. Thanks for your dedication and patience in teaching me the art of flying.

Mission #82 15 OCT 1944 to my teammates at Johns Hopkins University and the U.S. Olympic Lacrosse team of 1932, courtesy of Mr. Church Yearley.

Mission #84 18 OCT 1944 to My high school lacrosse coach and math teacher, Mr. D.A. Melosh, who recognized and supported my talents and interests and helped me push through an admitted lack of enthusiasm in my academic affairs and helped me become the player, student, and officer that I am today. Thank you, Coach!

Red Hawk moved the scene again, this time to the home of Jack's brother, Doug, as he received a letter from Colonel Finn.

28 Oct 1944

Mr. Douglas C. Turnbull, Jr.
Baltimore, Maryland

Dear Mr. Turnbull,

I write to share my grief in the loss of your beloved brother, Lt. Col. John I. "Jack" Turnbull. I had the good fortune to be assigned to Jack's Bomb Group in Shipdam, England. I must tell you that he was an incredibly talented officer, pilot, and leader. As flight surgeon for our group, I was tasked to perform the investigation into the accident that claimed Jack's life. The full report will not be released to for some months, I suspect, but I did want to share at least some preliminary details with you and your family.

I have sent a letter of condolence and Jack's personal belongings to your mother as Jack's next-of-kin indicated in his service record. That shipment should arrive in the coming days or weeks. She will receive all of the possessions found in Jack's lockers at Shipdam.

My report will state that the most likely cause of the crash was a midair collision between the plane Jack was on and another in their group. The entire formation was in a terrible thunderstorm—which they couldn't fly around or over. Two airmen were able to parachute out and reported that it seemed that the planes had clipped wings, causing each to go into an unrecoverable tailspin. Jack was serving as command pilot on one of the planes, which means that he was in charge of the entire formation but not actually at the controls of his aircraft. It seems to have been an unfortunate mishap that sometimes befalls our airmen in the conduct of such difficult and dangerous operations.

It is also with the deepest possible sense of humility to be the officer honored to be able to relay to you specifically upon Jack's request that this accompanying United States flag, wrapped in ribbons sent by his (and your) sister, Anne. Please remove the ribbons and unfurl the flag, and you will see two notes written by Jack. As you will see, Jack specifically requested that these items be sent to you for proper disposition.

Jack did not die in the crash—though the other twelve victims had—but valiantly fought for his life overnight in a nearby convent. He achieved only brief and intermittent moments of conscious-ness. The nuns who tended to Jack so passionately and dutifully say that Jack's last words—broken between long pauses early in the morning—were, "There are others. Please find. Please send. Thank you." Perhaps we should all be so lucky to be thinking of others and thanking people in our final moments.

I am also in the process of making arrangements to send similar flags and notes to the families of the other twelve airmen lost in this accident. Apparently Jack had made a plea to all of the airmen in his Bomb Group to consider incorporating this type of gesture of gratitude in all of their work and missions. It seems the men took the request to heart—literally.

I must tell you that I have never heard of such a gesture until this situation. Jack is said to have referred to the source of these tributes as one of the airmen assigned to the 44th Bomb Group—a sergeant D'Andrea, who, I regret to inform you, perished on the same mission as Jack and the eleven others. I intend to research this 'program' inspired by SGT D'Andrea in order to convey its tremendous significance to his family. I'll bet Jack took particular joy that this gesture was originated by one of the airmen in the group as opposed to an officer. Jack always had a particular fondness for the work and sacrifice of the enlisted men.

Though I simply cannot imagine how you will be able to properly conduct this request of your brother, I am certain that you will well and faithfully discharge your duty with the utmost dignity, sincerity, graciousness, and professionalism that would bring Jack great pride, joy, and honor.

Please accept my deepest condolences and best wishes that Jack's tributes to your mother, sisters, Mr. Carroll, Mr. Yearley and the rest of his team, Mr. Norris, and Mr. Melosh will leave a legacy of goodness, thoughtfulness, and gratitude that will adorn his already lustrous military career and heroic actions on behalf of our country. Please convey to the recipients my deepest sorrow on Jack's loss but also my deepest respect for him—and them for having contributed so meaningfully and powerfully to Jack's life and service.

Most Respectfully,

Drew J. Finn
Col., U.S. Army Air Corps

IT CAN ALL CHANGE
IN SECONDS

"Mark this, my young friend. Sear it into your soul with brands of iron: Never, never take anything for granted."

Alexander the Great in
The Virtues of War
Steven Pressfield

ROBBIE received an e-mail from Bruce which read: Robbie, I hope you are well. Attached are four letters that should be self-explanatory. I hope you will heed the sentiments of my father. Will be in touch soon. Be well. Bruce.

Robbie opened the attachments in order of date.

17 JUN 1955

Dear Mrs. Turnbull and Family,

Please accept my sincerest thanks for presenting the Lt.Col. John I. Turnbull Award to me in memory of your son. To have received it from you personally, in front of my parents, family, friends, and teammates—not to mention the 5,500 or so fans in attendance—at last week's North-South game at Homewood Field was certainly the highlight of my lacrosse career.

I am sure that you know better than I that this award represents the very pinnacle of the game of lacrosse. Many players in our game equate this honor to the Heisman Trophy given in football and none of us even dares to believe ourselves worthy. There were certainly many other players on the field that night that I thought would have been more deserving than me to receive this recognition.

Though I never played lacrosse in high school (my school did not offer it–so I played baseball!), it did not take me long to learn of the rich history of this game. To have a coach (Dinty Moore) like I have has been truly special as he has shared much of the deep meaning of the game with me, and the significance of Jack's (and Doug's) role in the history of the game.

Now that the Turnbull Award has been presented to me, I can only hope to represent it with the dignity and honor of my predecessors, and, of course, Jack himself.

I head off to flight school shortly. I will aspire to make you proud. My sincerest thanks.

Very Respectfully,
Percy Williams
ENS USN

June 21, 1955

Dear Percy,

Thank you for your kind letter of June 17. We are all thrilled by your selection for Jack's Award. I must say that your play in the North–South game was quite spectacular–four goals and two assists!–and reminded me so much of Jack–skilled, tenacious in your riding when your team lost the ball (Jack would have appreciated that the most), and great team play. I am certain that such play is representative of how you conduct all of your responsibilities and will translate very well and closely to your career as a navy pilot.

We have, of course, been so proud of each of the previous recipients, but your chosen path of taking to the skies in defense of our country gives my heart a little extra warmth.

Congratulations of your spectacular career to date and we

all wish you the very best as you head off to flight school. Our thoughts and prayers will be with you. I hope you will keep me posted of your endeavors.

Please convey to your parents my pleasure in speaking with them.

I hope that it is appropriate to wish you, "Fair Winds and Following Seas."

With Much Admiration and Gratitude,
Elizabeth Turnbull & Family

March 18, 1959

Dear Mr. and Mrs. Williams, Lee, and Jack,

It is with great sadness that I have learned of the loss of your son, husband, and father, Percy. Coach Moore called me last night. He and I are heartbroken over the loss of a truly remarkable young man. I know that my feeble words here will do little to ease your suffering but I if I can grant you even a second of solace, I will be glad of it.

I hope that you will recall our meeting at Homewood Field at the North-South game in June of 1955. Percy played a remarkable game.

At halftime, my (now) late mother, Elizabeth Turnbull, and I presented Percy with the Turnbull Award. We spoke with Percy briefly during the ceremony–then we all gathered for some time after the game. It was a great honor and pleasure meeting all of you. Your pride and joy in your son was clearly evident.

Percy sent our family a letter of thanks not long after the game–one that my mother cherished. I have included a copy here.

Your family's loss mirrors ours, if I might say. You, see, my brother Jack perished in an unfortunate plane crash, which was determined shortly after to not be attributable to his actions.

I understand from Coach Moore who was fully briefed by Navy officials as to the circumstances of the accident that it seems Percy's aircraft may have experienced a "flame out" of his engine and that his efforts to restart it were unsuccessful.

So our families are left to grieve the loss of two truly magnificent young men. We have taken solace over these last fifteen years in the knowledge that Jack was doing what he did best and loved most to do–fly planes in defense of our country.

And from our meeting with Percy and everything we have heard of him–his life seems remarkably similar.

For the Entire Turnbull Clan,
With Deepest Condolences,
Douglas C. Turnbull, Jr.

March 19, 1959

Dear Bruce,

I must share some sad news with you. You recall Percy Williams, the young man who received Jack's Award at the Naval Academy in 1955. I am sorry to report that he has perished in a navy plane crash off the USS *Intrepid* in the Atlantic Ocean near Gibraltar. I learned of this tragedy just today in a phone call from Percy's Naval Academy coach, Dinty Moore.

You'll see in the enclosed letter that my mother was extremely fond of Percy as he reminded her so much of Jack. She would be completely heartbroken to learn of this news were she still alive.

Coach Moore told me that LTJG Williams launched off the port catapult and it is believed he had a flame-out about a mile or so forward of the ship. It was guessed that he tried to restart his engine, which is why he didn't eject–but it was too late. The plane went into the sea, and sunk immediately. By the time the helicopters got there, there was no trace of the plane or pilot, not even an oil slick.

I think of Mum and the suffering she–and all of us–endured with Jack's loss. Percy's family will obviously suffer similarly. Percy, though, leaves behind a six-month-old son and a young wife expecting their second child. Please keep them all in your thoughts and prayers.

As I think of all of the lessons I have attempted to pass along to you–Percy's accident might represent the most central one: that life offers absolutely no guarantees and that everything for which you have worked so hard can change in seconds. This accident was certainly not the fault of Percy–yet he is gone.

My father used to tell us, "Don't take anything for granted." Sometimes things are outside of your immediate control. You can train and train and train for all situations–but sometimes you simply must yield to fate.

So I beg you to work hard to acquire the skills you need to be a great army officer and insist that those under your charge do the same. Teach them that they must prepare with the utmost resolve. But they must also understand that such work will certainly not guarantee their safety or successful completion of the specified mission. Those of you who have taken up the call of your country must know the perils inherent in such pursuits.

Jack and Percy knew it as they took to the skies. All mariners, submariners, and airmen know it. Everything can change in seconds–so work hard to ensure that you control everything you possibly can.

Don't take anything for granted.

Keep working hard to acquire every single ounce of knowledge you can.

With Love and Admiration for Your Pursuit of Leadership in the Armed Forces of our Country,

Dad

HE NEVER FORGOT
YOUR KINDNESS

"There is no wisdom greater than kindness."
Jean-Jacques Rousseau

O N the next full moon, Red Hawk and Robbie traveled through time to Baltimore, Maryland, December 1, 1944.

"Robbie, Doug has just received the letter from Col. Finn that we saw last time. As Jack requested, Doug is now about to personally deliver all of the flags to their recipients. His first decision was to meet with his sisters and mother. As you can see, they are just finishing dinner."

After dessert, Doug invited the entire family to his living room for an announcement. Mum, 'Libby,' Helen, and Anne and her husband Marshall McDorman sat close together.

"Thank you all for coming tonight. I have a short presentation that I would like to make on behalf of Jack," Doug began with solemnity.

The family began to look at each other in confused silence.

Doug continued, "Three days ago, I received a letter and package from the 44th Bomb Group's flight surgeon, Col. Drew Finn. Mother, this package is different from the one you received last week with Jack's personal effects from England. After I read Colonel Finn's letter to you, I was stunned to receive this separate letter and the contents of the package."

Doug read Col. Finn's letter aloud to the family. At various points, each family member wiped away tears from their eyes. Anne took it particularly hard.

"In addition to that letter were these notes that Jack had left in his foot locker and the ones on his person when he flew his final mission."

Doug read the first note–"Fly to Honor." As he read the part about the ribbons provided by Anne, she broke down in tears, struggling to catch her breath.

"Each of you has your own special flag and note from Jack." Doug walked slowly to each of his sisters and bent over to hug them, and present their flag and note. The women wept and pressed their flag and note to their chest. Finally, Doug presented the last flag and note to Mum.

"Jack included three other flags to be delivered, as well. I thought I would let you know who they were." Doug read each of them, once again eliciting more tears from everyone.

"I will plan to visit each of these good people in the coming week to present their flag to them. If any of you would like to come with me, I would be glad to have the company."

Anne immediately responded, "Doug, please let me come."

Red Hawk shared with Robbie that Doug and Anne had delivered all but the last flag and wanted Robbie to see that scene.

Doug and Anne arrived at the home of Mr. D. A. Melosh at 10 am on December 8, 1944, exactly as they had requested on the phone the day before.

"Good morning Doug, Anne, what a pleasure to see you. Please come in," Mr. Melosh offered. "You know my wife, Barbara."

"Yes, sir," Anne smiled. "So good to see you both. Thank you for having us." She handed a small floral arrangement to Mrs. Melosh.

"Oh, so nice. Thank you," Mrs. Melosh beamed. She hurried to her kitchen to get a vase and placed the flowers in it without missing a beat of the conversation.

The Meloshes offered tea and cookies to their guests and all sat down in the family living room.

"Barbara and I are so sorry for the loss of Jack. You know how well I have always thought of him," Mr. Melosh began. "Please convey our deepest condolences to your mother and sisters, once again, would you?"

"Yes, sir," Doug answered, "Thank you. You were always so good to him. He always told us that you understood him more than all of his other teachers. Our family is so grateful for all of your efforts on his behalf."

"It was truly an honor, Doug. I think I may have been a bit more sensitive to Jack than some others because I shared his, should we say, lack of excitement for academic pursuits, at about the same age."

"Yes—I think we can say that," Doug agreed with a smile.

"Mr. Melosh, we are here today to offer a tribute that Jack made to you during his time in the Army Air Corps," Anne said.

The Meloshes looked at each other silently.

Doug unsnapped the briefcase he had brought with him and removed the letter that Lt. Col. Finn had sent to him. He read it to the Meloshes who continued their silence.

Then Anne read the "Fly to Honor" note. Still total silence.

Then Doug read the personal note to them.

"This is the actual flag that Jack had on his person on his final flight," Doug whispered and knelt as he offered it to Mr. Melosh, who now began to weep. "He wanted you to have it. He dedicated other flights in similar fashion, as did his entire crew under Jack's encouragement. But Anne and I could not agree more that his final flight should have been dedicated to you for all you have done for him. We can't thank you enough."

Melosh paused for several moments, so overcome with emotion. He wiped back his tears and took a few slow breaths. "I really don't know what to say, Doug," Mr. Melosh stammered. "I was a teacher for forty years and I have never been so moved by a gesture. Oh, my goodness." He looked at his wife, who was sobbing softly into a handkerchief.

"I was an army officer myself and have never heard of anything like this. I am eighty years old. I have never heard of this before. I don't know what to say."

"We didn't know about any of this either. You don't need to say anything," eased Anne. "Just know that Jack was grateful to you—and we are sure hundreds and hundreds of other young men are, as well. He will never forgot your kindness. Thank you."

Robbie and Red Hawk waved goodbye to each other with a word.

LEGACY

"Every child should have someone, somewhere,
who will do something for them that makes no sense
but is absolutely magical."

Guy Friddell

ROBBIE, his sister, and his parents met Captain Lewis, Bruce and Jerri Turnbull, and Bob Scott at Coach Scott's home in Baltimore.

"Robbie, Catherine, John, and Mary, thank you for coming today. Bruce, Jerri, and I wanted to present a special gift to Robbie and Catherine," Scott began.

He pulled out a handsome wooden box and opened it to reveal two photo albums, each decoratively covered with a United States flag.

Jerri began, "Catherine, I'd like to you to have this album. It is a collection of letters from Jack to Anne. She kept them all in a shoebox for many years and then put them into this beautiful album which Bruce will describe shortly."

Jerri handed the album to the girl with a gentle hug. Her heart glowed as she watched Catherine delicately flip through the dozens of letters. The girl's life, Jerri though, was about to be enriched in ways she couldn't even imagine, like Robbie's.

"I think you'll see what a little sister means to a big brother–Jack let her know it all the time," Jerri added while offering Robbie a smile as a plea for him to tell his sister how special she was to him.

Coach Scott then addressed the boy, "Robbie, I have taken the liberty of soliciting each of the Turnbull Award recipients over the last sixty-five years to send you a note. I made a pretty simple request and got a fantastic response. I asked them to share some thoughts with you the 'old-school' way—a letter as opposed to an e-mail! I think this collection will have a nice, personal feel for you. About fifty have responded and they are included in this album."

Bruce added, "Robbie, Catherine, I'd like to point out the albums, themselves. You can see that the cover looks very much like a shadow box—though these are made of fabric—that might be used to house valuables and are often used to commemorate military service. Jack's sister Anne, who was quite a talented artist, made the albums herself. She designed a large plastic pocket to hold the flag and then sewed the pocket into the beautiful wood-colored fabric border and wrapped it around the album. The strings securing the album are the ones that actually held Jack's flags—the ones she sent to him wrapping many gifts. The first one, Catherine, was made from the flag Jack actually carried on a combat mission designated to honor Anne. She kept the album with the letters in it on her nightstand her whole life. She left it all to me in her will."

Robbie's parents felt a chill go through their bodies.

"Robbie," Bruce continued, "your album was also made by Anne, but the flag in yours was the one carried by Jack on his fateful last mission and was later sent to his coach at Poly, Mr. Melosh. Several years after Doug and Anne presented the flag and note to him, he passed away. His wife graciously returned the flag to my father and he gave it to Anne to mount on this album. It had been empty all these years. When Coach Scott informed me of his intention to collect letters from all of the recipients of Uncle Jack's Award for you, I suggested that we use this album. We all hope that you will enjoy and learn from it."

Scott read the dedication page to Robbie and his family, "In life, Jack Turnbull was an inspiration to all with whom he came into contact. Even in his death, Jack continued to give to people, and now his Awards continue to represent excellence in the game of lacrosse. This collection of letters is offered to Robbie with great admiration and on behalf of scores of Turnbull Award recipients, Robert H. Scott. July 2014."

Scott then read his own letter to the group.

Robbie's parents, who thought they could not be any more overwhelmed than they had been in the previous year, reached yet another level of surprise and gratitude. Coach Scott invited the adults to adjourn to the kitchen area for soft drinks and snacks as to allow the children the time to enjoy their new treasures.

After about twenty minutes, the children returned to the group, a bit stunned and overwhelmed.

Bruce beamed at Robbie and Catherine, "I hope you'll enjoy those albums. What do you think?"

"I love it. But this is way too much for me to keep to myself. I have to think of a way to share this with other people," Robbie said gratefully. "Thank you, Coach Scott!"

"If you are able to do that, Robbie that would be a great gift from you to the Game. You know what? I may have an idea...."

[Author's note: For the benefit of the layout of this volume, the entire collection of letters in Robbie's album is presented at the back of this book.]

Epilogue

"Give a child a book and you change the world–maybe even the universe."

Neil deGrasse Tyson
"Cosmos: A Spacetime Odyssey"

The Lacrosse Museum and Hall of Fame, Baltimore, Maryland

"WHAT a great idea, Coach," Jim Lewis said to Bob Scott as they waited along with Robbie, his parents, and Bruce and Jerri Turnbull for several dozen guests to arrive at the Lacrosse Museum and Hall of Fame, adjacent to US Lacrosse Headquarters and Homewood Field.

"Well, Jim, I just thought it would be fun to get all of these guys and their families together in honor of Jack and Robbie–and the little treat we have in mind should be fun. It should be quite a night," Coach Scott smiled.

Some twenty five or thirty Turnbull Award recipients made their way into the Museum over the next thirty or so minutes with their guests–parents, coaches, wives, girlfriends, children–about one hundred people in all, each greeting Coach Scott, Captain Lewis, Bruce and Jerri, and Robbie as they arrived.

It was an incredible sight. Players from seven or eight decades glowing in each other's presence, all genuinely thrilled and grateful to be there. The emotion in the room was palpable. People were glancing at nametags, erupting into joyful laughter, handshakes, hugs, and even a tear or two, and posing for pictures for their wives. Dozens of the greatest ever to play the game were simply enjoying each other. If it ever was about them—it wasn't any more. Tonight it was about the game, the friendships, the future. This event was about passing along their experience to young players, to each other, and the game itself.

Some of the greats were teammates with each other along their journey; some had played in the same recreation league, middle school, high school, college, club, or professional teams, and even on the same or different USA (or other nations') national teams— together or decades apart. Some had played with or against each other many times through the years. Coach Scott scanned the group, beaming with joy as he absorbed the radiance of the room. What a collection of talent, personality, and wonderful, hard-working, generous people, he mused.

The US Lacrosse staff was there to welcome everyone, guiding them to drinks and appetizers set up around the Museum. The staff had meticulously arranged a special exhibit about Jack Turnbull specifically for them. The area contained several scrap books arranged by Jack's nephew and Bruce's brother (also) Jack Turnbull and a video projector scrolling through scores of pictures from Jack's life, lacrosse career, military service and, ultimately, grave. The beautiful album Coach Scott had presented to Robbie was also on display— drawing each contributor to inspect all of the letters it contained in addition to theirs, while also viewing the pictures of Jack and the other scrapbooks and mementos.

Of greatest interest to all in attendance, though, was Robbie's stick, which he held with him as he was introduced to the guests. As each Award recipient greeted Robbie, the boy instantly connected them to their letter. Without exception, each Award recipient graciously accepted Robbie's offer to inspect the stick. In remarkably similar and reverent fashion, each legend did nearly the same thing— they took the stick in their hands and felt its balance. They ran their fingers along the wood, twirled it ever so slowly, looked at it long ways, inspected the carvings and writing, gently cradled it, ran their fingers along it again, softly cradled it once more, and handed it back to Robbie. Each could feel the stick's magic they had heard about, and were instantaneously drawn back to the special feeling that had existed in their stick—a feeling that had captivated and driven them—during their playing days.

After about an hour of mingling and rekindling old friendships, Lewis announced to the group, "Good evening, ladies and gentlemen. Thank you for coming. We hope you will enjoy tonight's program and your particular role in it.

"I would like to thank US Lacrosse for hosting us today. Mostly, I'd like to thank Coach Scott for what he has meant to the game and all of us for all these years and particularly this event tonight."

Each Turnbull Award recipient immediately broke into applause. Scott attempted to wave off the recognition—but it continued for several minutes.

Lewis finally continued, "All of you know the main purpose of why we have gathered tonight—that part will come later. But we also have a little surprise for you out on Homewood Field—so please make your way out there. We'll meet back in here after the game. Enjoy."

The group moved out to the field where each Turnbull recipient received an index card with a young player's name and number on it and was directed by the US Lacrosse staff to either end of the field where teams were meeting for a pregame ceremony—half on one end, half on the other. Most of the recipients noticed the special arrangement of players and parents, so they edged in eagerly. Each group was conducting their own ceremony. Robbie's coach began by addressing his team.

"Ladies and gentlemen, thank you for coming tonight. We think we have a very special evening planned for you. We will begin here with a 'Play to Honor' recognition for our team. Then we'll have a game with the Tigers. After the game, we'll ask you to meet us in the Hall of Fame right over there for another short ceremony.

"Our boys were encouraged to invite a person who has impacted their life in a positive way to be their guest of honor tonight. This gesture was initiated by one of our own players–Robbie–to model a story of which he had learned recently. Robbie and I visited the Tigers a couple weeks ago and asked them to consider conducting a similar ceremony for their team, which they are doing on the other end of the field. We picked the Tigers specifically because their coach and I were teammates many years ago.

"You may also notice that the referees are also holding a similar ceremony with their group at midfield. They are calling their part, 'Referee to Honor.' We hope you will agree that this is a remarkably simple–but, hopefully, powerful gesture that gives our boys an opportunity to formally thank someone special in their life, and play a game in someone's honor. We'll invite each boy to recognize their 'Play to Honoree.'"

The boys introduced their honorees, one by one, with a sentence or two to convey the nature of the relationship they had with their special guests.

Robbie began, "My 'Play to Honoree' is Captain Jim Lewis. Jim played for Navy back in the '60s and is in the Hall of Fame. He has shared a very special old stick with me and has supported me more than I can believe over the last couple years."

The boys continued by introducing themselves and their honorees.

"I'm Bobby and my 'Play to Honoree' is my grandfather, John Rowe, who has been to every one of my games since I can remember."

"I'm Bill and my 'Play to Honoree' is my math teacher, Miss Dempsey, who helped me every day on my free period."

"I'm Scott and my 'Play to Honoree' is my mom, Arlette, because…well, she's my mom."

"I'm Andy. My 'Play to Honoree' is my uncle, Joe Drost, who taught me a lot about how to play and comes to all of my games."

"I'm Danny and my 'Play to Honorees' are my athletic trainers, Antoinette, Julie, and Lauren, who helped me recover from and rehab my injury last year."

"I'm John and my 'Play to Honorees' are my sisters Christine, Moira, and Lauren."

"I'm Dave and my 'Play to Honoree' is my football coach, Mr. Snyder."

The rest of the boys continued in similar fashion.

Most of the guests and parents had no idea that they were to be so honored–the e-mail Robbie's coach had sent out said only that they were invited to attend a "Short, but Special Ceremony"–and were clearly moved by the gesture. Coach Scott had not briefed the Turnbull Award recipients (except one) on this part of the program and they also watched in joy as the young men publicly thanked their special guest. Their thoughts quickly flew back to their life at age fifteen and chuckled at themselves that they were hardly able to tie their shoes at that point–no less speak so well and with such genuine gratitude.

After each boy and coach had honored their guest, Robbie's coach concluded the ceremony. "Thank you all for coming. I hope you see why we are so proud of these boys. Thank you for what you have meant to these players. I hope the boys will find just a little extra energy to put forth for their team and will do you appropriate honor. Enjoy the game. We'll see you after the game in the Museum. Let's get to work, boys."

The teams played a spirited and hard-fought game. Each coach made it a special point to ensure a good amount of playing time for each player and they were thrilled by the terrific effort from each boy.

All of the people in attendance knew that the actual outcome of the game was important–the Tigers ended up winning 7-6–but that the most important part of the evening had already happened–the tributes to the honored guests–or at least that's what they thought.

After the players had taken off their gear and washed up they convened in the Museum.

When all had finally gathered, Roddy Marino addressed the crowd, "Ladies and gentlemen, thank you for coming tonight. I am Roddy Marino, and I have the honor of welcoming you here. I hope that you all enjoyed the pregame ceremonies and the game itself. We gather now to enjoy each other and for one more special part of tonight's program. You see, tonight's entire event was inspired by Robbie in very large part due to his relationship with Captain Jim Lewis, Navy '66, who has passed down a special stick to him. Jim, would you wave? Robbie has learned quite a bit about the game and some of the players who had the stick before Jim.

"One of those people was none other than Lieutenant Colonel Jack Turnbull of the World War II Army Air Corps. Jack was a three-time First-Team All-American here at Hopkins—playing on that very same field these boys just played on—and Hall of Fame member. He was a pilot who lost his life in the war, but is remembered today in several forms. One is the Turnbull Award which is presented annually to the most outstanding attackman in each of the three college divisions. The actual trophy is housed here in the Museum." Marino gestured to the US Lacrosse staff member standing by the five-foot-high glassed-in trophy case, as the guests looked on in deep admiration.

"I am proud to say that I am one such recipient—all the way back in 1986 at the University of Virginia," Marino offered a bit sheepishly as he was normally impeccably modest, but since Coach Scott had asked him to emcee this part of the program there was no escaping a bit of self-reference.

"The ceremony that you witnessed on the field was very much modeled on a gesture by Lt. Col. Turnbull, who carried a flag of the United States in honor of people who had supported him. He called it, 'Fly to Honor.' The recipients of those tributes received them after Jack's death in 1944. Though these boys are not able to dedicate an actual combat mission, we hope that you enjoyed the similarity of their offering to you.

"Gathered around us here tonight are dozens of my fellow Turnbull Award recipients–or family representatives–going back all the way to 1946. Some came from great distances to be with us–so we thank them for the effort to be here. You can identify them by their nametags. You may also be able to identify them by their picture on the wall in the Hall of Fame around that corner–or maybe not," Roddy joked in regard to their old age, drawing more than a few chuckles from his brethren.

"A few could not make this event, but have offered their support to these players. If your Turnbull Award recipient is not here–please meet with Jack's nephews Bruce and Jack Turnbull and their wives Jerri and Jane right there," Roddy nodded. "They will be glad to provide you some information on your person.

"In tribute to the wonderful relationship that has arisen from Jim's kind gesture in passing his stick to Robbie, Coach Scott has asked each of us to bring one of our sticks to pass down to these youngsters here tonight and we are genuinely thrilled and honored to be able to participate."

Everyone in the room began to look around in disbelief and amazement, wondering what was about to happen and who all of the great players might be.

Roddy addressed the young players, "Boys, your coaches have prepared a list of 'connections' between you and a Turnbull recipient. We would ask you, your parents, and your 'Play to Honoree' to please introduce yourselves to the Turnbull recipient I will name. We will not have a formal close tonight–so please just take a few minutes to get to know each other. Let me quickly introduce each Turnbull recipient and we would ask you to make your way to them. Thank you all for coming tonight. Enjoy!"

The young players and their parents beamed with excitement as Roddy read off the list and then they hurried to meet their new friends.

Lewis and Scott scanned the introductions and discussions taking place around the room. The joy on both sides–the youngsters and parents as well as the Turnbull recipients–was overwhelming.

Most of the discussions followed a similar line–the legend providing a brief–and far-too-modest–biography, including their hometown, college, year they received the Award, etc.

But the legends diverted the discussion away from themselves as quickly as they could and asked the boys to tell them about themselves, their families, their "Play to Honoree," and their team. From the cards handed to them, each knew in advance the player with whom they would be connecting so they had carefully watched them play and spoke with detail–starting with their jersey number!–about how well they played during the game. The boys and their parents were overwhelmed with pride, joy, and gratitude for the connection with these men.

At some point in the discussions, each legend handed their player a stick they had once used on the field. The sticks covered the entire range of the history of the game–from sixty-year-old wooden ones to the modern day plastic versions, custom dyed with school, professional, and even a few USA, Canada, Australia, and Wales national colors. The legends also provided their young men with a copy of the book they had recommended to Robbie, also on Scott's request. They handed the parents a card with their contact information. Most wrapped up the discussion with a pledge to follow up and stay in contact.

After all of the guests had drifted out of the Museum, Scott could still feel the electricity in the air. He had attended hundreds of events similar to this one but this had been different, he thought. His heart glowed, perhaps more than it had in quite some time, its warmth slowly seeping into his imagination.

Knowing so many of the Turnbull recipients personally, and the players they were and the people they had become, he already had a clear vision of what the next phase of Jack's legacy might look like.

"Thanks, Jim," he whispered to Captain Lewis.

SPECIAL THANKS

The depth and breadth of my gratitude on this project is several orders of magnitude greater, even, than for *The Spirit in the Stick*. The sheer number of people involved with and the volume of goodness that has been entrusted to me for *Fly to Honor* is far more than I can adequately convey here.

Once again, this project would not have been possible if not for the gracious and positive support of many people. First and foremost, CAPT Jim Lewis, USNA '66, MAJ R. Bruce and Jerri Turnbull, USMA '57, Jack and Jane Turnbull, and Susan Generazio, who were gracious in offering information, and latitude with their lives as well as the lives of their relatives.

It would not have been possible to include every award received by many of the generous contributors to this effort, which would have included at least *sixteen* Division I USILA Coach of the Year awards, and numerous school, and US Lacrosse Chapter Halls of Fame, etc. For the most part, I have restricted the identifications to USILA "Special" awards and "Tewaaraton" Awards.

Bob Scott (2013 *"Spirit of Tewaaraton"* Award recipient) has continued to be a source of inspiration and support of this project for fifteen years.

I would like to thank my high school coach, Don Holmes, for the positive impact he has had on my life. I must thank my high school teammates and classmates, who were also my college classmates, Bill Dempsey and Dave Gallaer, USNA '84.

It was extremely gratifying for me to receive the support and participation of Dick Szlasa and Dr. Bryan Matthews, my coaches at the Naval Academy.

I am grateful for the friendship and support of all of my teammates at the United States Naval Academy, and I am particularly grateful for the career service of scores of them (attempting to list them all here will certainly result in an error).

I could not be more honored to have Army Lacrosse coaches Jim Adams, Peg Pisano for Al Pisano, Dick Edell (2010 *"Spirit of Tewaaraton"* Award recipient), Jack Emmer, and Joe Alberici–56 straight years of USMA coaching–provide the Introduction. Incredible! Thank you!

Once again, Mike Gottleib, USNA '70, provided inspired artwork and layout for the cover. Jonathan Gullery did another excellent job with the layout of the text. Thanks to Jacki Lynch and Ron Pramschufer at BooksJustBooks.com. Kelly Jackson Higgins provided excellent editing assistance at a critical point.

I am also grateful for the assistance of: Lynn Paul of Norfolk Academy, Joe Finn of US Lacrosse, John Spring of the USILA, Neil Grauer and Ernie LaRossa of Johns Hopkins, Fred Rasmussen, Steven Goldburg, Wayne Johnson, Chris Davis, Bobby Reinhart, my fellow lacrosse coaches–Tom Duquette, Michael Via, Jack Gibson, Witt Borum, Steve Monninger, Trent Blythe, J. Sills O'Keefe, Greg Barton, Hannon Wright, and my many colleagues at Norfolk Academy.

I continue to be grateful for the support of Steve Stenersen of US Lacrosse, Bob Carpenter and John Jiloty of *Inside Lacrosse*, and Sarah Aschenbach of the Tewaaraton Foundation.

I am grateful and humbled by the generous testimonials of: Dom Starsia (Virginia), Sid Jamieson (Bucknell) (2005 *"Spirit of Tewaaraton"* Award recipient), Mike Hanna (Hobart), Mike Murphy (Colgate), J.P. Stewart (Virginia Wesleyan), Steve Koudelka (Lynchburg), and Ray Rostan (Hampden-Sydney), and Erin Quinn (Middlebury).

Thanks also to Richie Moran (2012 *"Spirit of Tewaaraton"*

Award recipient), Mark Johnson and Eric Steffen (Wisconsin), Jim Berkman (Salisbury), Chris Bates (Princeton), Greg Raymond and Jerry Fisk (Hobart), Jeff Long (Ithaca), Jason Archbell (Bowdoin), Tom Gill (USMMA), Dave Webster (Dickinson), Jonathan Thompson (Amherst), Mike Daly (Tufts), Jake Coon (RIT), Steve Beville (Cortland), Rob Randall (Nazareth), Hillary Fisher (Johns Hopkins), J.B. Clarke (Limestone), Dan Sheehan (LeMoyne), Chris Ryan (Mercyhurst), and Bill Pilat (Roanoke).

Special thanks also to Shannon Revell, USNA '04, and Giovanna Kastrubala, USNA '95 and their wonderful initiative, "Run to Honor," as well as Buddy Garland, USNA '84, Sam Dorrence, Ryan Mita, Jacklyn Sassa, and Callie Oettinger.

The Lacrosse Story by Alexander M. Weyand and Milton R. Roberts H. & A. Herman and the Garamond/Pridemark Press, Baltimore, Maryland, 1965, was extremely helpful.

I am immensely grateful to all of the Turnbull Award recipients who participated in this project, including: Stewart McLean, W. Brooke Tunstall and his wife, Peg, and their daughters Tricia, Paige, and Leslie, Bill Stutt, USNA '49 and the family of J.H.L. Chambers '49, Don, Pam, and Tobin Hahn, Jeff Shepard, Bill Tanton, C. Rennie Smith, the family and friends of Percy Williams, USNA '55, Jack Williams, Lee Hual, CAPT Shannon Heyward, USNA '57, CAPT Jack Renard '55, Fred Tolleson, USNA '55, Johns Jaudon USNA '55, RADM Andy Wilkinson, USNA '57, my former coach Dr. Bryan Matthews and the family of Dr. Hezzy Howard, Jack Daut, Dick Corrigan, Bill Morrill, Bob Miser, USMA '60, Tom Mitchell, USNA '61, my former coach Dick Szlasa and Olga Schmidt, Ray and Janice Altman, CAPT Jim Lewis, USNA '66, Joe Cowan, Tom Cafaro, USMA '71, John Kaestner, Jack Thomas, John "Jake" O'Neill and the family of Eamon McEneaney, Michael French, Michael O'Neill, Bob Boneillo, Mike Buzzell, USNA '80, Mrs. Anne Lee Huether, Craig Cook, Tim Nelson, Roddy Marino, Tim Goldstein, John Zulberti, Greg Burns, Mark Douglas, Darren Lowe, Matt Riter, Terry Riordan, Michael Watson, Jon Hess, Casey Powell, Ryan

Powell, Matt Danowski, Rob Pannell, Steele Stanwick, Bob Engelke, Rob Grella, Mark Mangan, Gavin Chamberlain, Nick Carlson, Greg Cerar, Jack Harmatuk, Jack Venditti, Brian Scheetz, Rick Gilbert, Bob Griebe, Terry Corcoran, Roy McAdam, Jeff Kauffman, Paul Goldsmith, Marc Van Arsdale, Ray Gilliam, Tom Gravante, Bill Miller, Tim Hormes, Marty Kelly, Cabell Maddux, Jason Coffman, Dave Maguire, Darren McGurn, Joe High, Jon Fellows, Josh Bergey, Michael Saraceni, Ryan Hotaling, Dan Boyer, Jon Mason, Ryan Heath, DJ Hessler, Matt Cannone, and Brian Cannon.

As always, I owe the largest debt of gratitude to my wife, partner, and best friend, Jennifer, who for many years has patiently indulged my passion for the game of lacrosse and no less a passion for my students. It continues to go without saying that our children, Catherine and Drew, are the central source of hope and happiness in our lives.

As with *The Spirit in the Stick*, this project could have easily withered or died at many points. I was heartened and buoyed by the overwhelming and timely acts of kindness by all of these wonderful people. The completion of this project is as much a tribute to the generosity of others as it is to any of my humble efforts.

This journey continues to be its own reward. The fact that you have taken it with me makes it all the more special.

Thank you.

ABOUT THE AUTHOR

NEIL Duffy is a native of Massapequa Park, Long Island. He is a graduate of Alfred G. Berner High School, the United States Naval Academy, and Old Dominion University. He is a teacher, coach, and advisor at Norfolk Academy in Norfolk, Virginia and he is the author of *The Spirit in the Stick*. He resides in Virginia Beach with his wife, daughter, and son.

Please share your thoughts and criticisms with the author at www.thespiritinthestick.com.

LETTERS TO ROBBIE

In life, Jack Turnbull was an inspiration to all with whom he came into contact. Even in his death, Jack continued to give to people, and now his Awards continue to represent excellence in the game of lacrosse.

This collection of letters is offered to Robbie with great admiration and on behalf of scores of Turnbull Award recipients,

Robert H. Scott
July 2014

Dear Turnbull Award recipient,

I write to invite you to share some thoughts with a special young boy, Robbie, who is turning fifteen years old and is a ninth-grader.

I recently met Robbie and his family through his association with Captain Jimmy Lewis, Navy '66. Robbie is now in possession of a special and magical lacrosse stick that Jim passed along to him and which was passed to him by Doug Turnbull, Johns Hopkins '25. The stick had been passed to Doug in 1914 and he eagerly shared it with his brother, Jack (which is where you all come into this story).

As incredible as it may seem, through the stick Robbie has been 'visited' in his dreams on every full moon by a Native American named Red Hawk who was the original steward of the stick in the late 1700s! Robbie has already learned a great deal from Red Hawk and CAPT Lewis. But I write to you, as a recipient of the Lt. Col. John I. "Jack" Turnbull Award, to help Robbie in his journey to know more about the stick and the game.

I would be grateful if you would write a letter to Robbie so that I may collect them and place them in a special album for him. Please address any thoughts you would like—but perhaps you could offer a very brief mention of your playing and/or coaching background, what the Turnbull Award has meant to you, any particularly compelling memories of the game, and perhaps some advice on the game or on life. If you have had to overcome any particularly difficult situation or obstacle, it might be useful to share that, as well.

In addition—I would be grateful if you might offer a recommendation on a book that you think might benefit him at this stage of his life. Please do not be modest about what differentiated your game or identifying your status as a Hall of Fame member, team USA (or other country), etc.

Thanks for taking the time to help this young man—I know that he will be overwhelmed by and benefit from your kindness.

Yours in the Game,

Robert H. Scott

Dear Robbie,

I hope that you will enjoy this collection as much as I have. These men are truly among the all-time great *players*. But, as you'll see, they are all hard-working and wonderful *people*, as well. I think their eagerness in responding says a lot not only about them but also about our great Game. So many of us who have been involved with the Game all these years will tell you it has always been about the people. I think that theme shines through in this collection. I hope that you'll be able to use the lives and thoughts of these great men as an inspiration as you live your life. Some of the letters are on behalf of the Award recipients who have passed away. I was able to connect with people close to them who were equally gracious in their responses.

In all the years I have been involved with the Game, I would have to put the generosity of spirit offered by these men at the very top of the list. I think it is a great gift from the Game to you. I hope you will enjoy it! Thank you for allowing me to travel with you on your journey.

I have made a few editorial comments on these letters to share some thoughts and information that you may not know or might not be obvious.

With Warmest Regards,

Robert H. Scott

To: Robbie
From: Bill Morrill

Dear Robbie,

My college coach, Bob Scott, has asked me to share with you some of my experiences playing lacrosse some fifty years ago.

I was fortunate to grow up in a lacrosse family. My father played for Hopkins in the 1920s, then coached there in the 1930s, '40s, and '50s. He played with Doug Turnbull and coached Jack Turnbull.

I never knew Jack Turnbull, but Doug was an active supporter of Hopkins Lacrosse. He was a true role model for us because he was not only a great player, but a successful businessman and community leader.

As a result of my knowledge of the Turnbull legacy, my receipt of the Turnbull Award in 1959 was particularly gratifying to my family and me.

As I think back on my playing days, there are several things that I was taught that helped me compete at a high level.

My father insisted that I learn to play right and left handed. Today, everyone plays with both hands. But with the heavy, unbalanced sticks of the 1950s, I was one of the very few who could play equally well with both hands. My father also insisted that I work hard on both athletics and academics. Finally, he taught me to love and respect the game of lacrosse and to give back to it after my playing days were through.

Bill Nichols, my coach at Baltimore Friends, taught me that you had to play with courage and be willing to take a hit to score, get ground balls, and win.

Bob Scott and Wilson Fewster, my coaches at Hopkins, pushed me to make up for my thin frame and lack of sprint speed by working extremely hard on improving my quickness, my change of direction, and my shooting. I spent hours in the off-season and after practice working on my stickwork, dodges, change of direction, quickness, and shooting.

In addition, like Captain Lewis, who passed the magic stick along to you, I spent hours trying to come up with new ways to hold my stick, pass, dodge, and shoot.

Finally, and probably most important, I played on really good teams with great teammates. From them, I learned the value commitment, discipline, passion, respect, and responsibility. I also formed great relationships (with teammates and opponents) that have lasted a lifetime.

In his letter to me, Coach Scott asked me to recommend a book that could be of benefit to you. I would suggest you read *Values of the Game* by Bill Bradley, a basketball star at Princeton and the NBA, a Rhodes Scholar, an Olympian, as well as a three-time U.S. Senator. Bill Bradley combined hard work and dedication to overachieve in academics, athletics, and in his professional career.

Robbie, you are at the beginning of an exciting career. Lacrosse is a wonderful sport that is fun to practice as well as play. The things you will learn and the relationships you will make will be important you throughout your life. I wish you great success and hope that you enjoy the game as much as I have.

Yours in the Game,

Bill Morrill

Johns Hopkins University
Turnbull Award 1959
National Lacrosse Hall of Fame, Class of 1978

Robbie,

Congratulations to you for being chosen by Captain Lewis to receive the magical lacrosse stick. The fact that he selected you for this honor is a compliment to your qualities as a young man. So what responsibility do you have as the recipient of this wonderful gift? As a former player and coach who grew up in Mt. Washington and lived on Sulgrave Ave., just down the street from where Jack Turnbull was raised, I would like to share a few thoughts for you to consider.

Success in life, as in lacrosse, is not an automatic. It requires dedication and commitment. I must confess that as a 15 year old, I did not fully appreciate the magnitude of these qualities. It wasn't until later in life when I became a parent, coach and businessman that I fully understood the importance. My advice to you is to enhance the power of the stick and develop your own magic by making the commitment to become the best lacrosse player you can be. Formulate a plan by listing everything you must learn to perfection from scooping, passing, catching, shooting, dodging and all the fundamentals of the game. Implement the plan by listening to your coaches, reading, watching star players, and studying DVD's.

Become a student of the game. For example, take the one category of dodging. List at least eight dodges to learn, (face, inside roll, split, rocker, etc.) Know when to use them, how to bait the opposing player, where to hold and move the stick, plus footwork. Once you have your plan, go for it. Monitor your progress and make changes as necessary. It may take several years, but I know you will reap the rewards. One of my favorite examples of the success of commitment is the book *Undaunted Courage* by Stephen E. Ambrose. It details the journey of Lewis and Clark across the continent to discover a passage to the west and the impediments they faced.

In summary, Robbie, the power of the magic in the stick is directly relational to the commitment of the player possessing the stick. Good luck to you and enjoy the journey.

Sincerely,

Tom Mitchell

United States Naval Academy, Turnbull Award 1961

Dear Robbie,

I was happy to hear that you are taking great care of a very special lacrosse stick. While lacrosse is an amazing sport that requires skill, athleticism, and strategy, dating back to the Indian tribes who invented the game, lacrosse has also always had a significant spiritual side to it that you are no doubt getting a sense for by now. Lacrosse, for me, has been much more than simply a sport. It has taught me toughness, perseverance, and humility, and its lessons have also prepared me for the many ups and downs in life that I have had to face off with.

Like that stick that has been passed down to you with a story, as lacrosse players we are mentored and taught by those that came before us. There is a phrase I have been taught that I would like to share with you; I hope it helps to influence some of your decisions and your respect of the game. It goes like this... "We stand on the shoulders of those who came before us." While the many individual accolades I have received throughout my career have been rewarding and humbling, none of them compare to the feeling of being a part of a team...part of a winning team with a sense of destiny and/or legacy...part of a winning team in this great sport of Lacrosse or 'Baggataway.' I am most proud of the Championship Teams I was blessed to have played on and the respect we were able to show those players before us who had paved the way for our success.

Enjoy that special and spiritual stick and listen to the many lessons it will teach you. And pick up one of my favorite books, *My Personal Best*, by John Wooden. John Wooden was a remarkable teacher, coach and mentor of young men and his UCLA Men's Basketball Teams won 10 NCAA National Championships in 12 years. I hope you enjoy Coach Wooden's life lessons and fun stories as much as I have.

All the best,

Billy Miller

Hobart College, Turnbull Award 1989, 1991
Philadelphia Wings '92–'98
USA World Team '94, '98
National Lacrosse Hall of Fame, Class of 2013

Dear Robbie,

I am glad to respond to Coach Scott's invitation to share some of my lacrosse experience with you. I grew up in Baltimore and began playing with the Mount Washington juniors and then I played at Poly and the University of Maryland. I followed the example of my brothers Jim, Gene, and George Corrigan.

Receiving the Turnbull Award was very special for me. I knew Jack was a fantastic player at Hopkins and Mount Washington, but, more importantly, I knew that he was admired and respected by all who knew him. I am still humbled to have received the Turnbull Award after all these years—there are so many fine players. But since I have been involved in the game for so long now I should say that it was a great moment in a lifetime of great memories.

After I graduated from Maryland, I began a long and very rewarding career in coaching. I felt like I was very fortunate to have the coaches I did—Bill McLean at Poly and Jack Faber and Al Heagy at Maryland. Coach Faber was particularly influential. He had a very basic philosophy about the game—Loose Balls Win Games, Pass and Cut, Always Move on Offense, and Be Physical on Defense. He recognized the talents of his players and let them play. I loved him and I was blessed by being able to play for him. He was a Ph. D. microbiologist and a very unique man—though he refused to allow us to call him "doctor."

My own coaching career took me to Navy (offensive coordinator), Yale (head coach), the USILA Rules Committee, Governor Dummer (head coach), and I'm still coaching at Worcester Prep in Berlin, Maryland (assistant coach). My mind is full of names and faces and great memories of the young men I have coached. I feel like I have won the jackpot—a great playing experience and a great coaching experience. One experience that is probably at the top was that I got to coach with Willis Bilderback and Buster Phipps at Navy during the beginning of their long run of national championships. Coach Bilderback allowed me—as a twenty-five-year-old assistant coach—to handle all of his offense! More importantly than that, though, was that he and his family invited me over for dinner every Sunday night while I was there and made me a part of their family— what an incredible coach and even better person!

I've won a few national championships, coached some truly great men, and created lifetime friendships. I cried for those (from Navy in the early 60s) who died in Vietnam.

Some advice I might pass along is to enjoy the game, love your teammates (they will likely be lifelong friends), and honor the game–not yourself. I do remember a player who said that awards such as the Turnbull were good for the Game as it was a motivation factor that enhanced the competitive nature of the Game. I think I agree with that observation.

At this age, Robbie, I don't remember all of the specific details of my playing and coaching career. I do remember, though, that several years ago one of my former players, who is now a retired four-star U.S. Navy admiral, Hank Chiles, said to me, "Thank you for the way you (Coach Bilderback, Coach Phipps, and myself at Navy) coached us." If that were all I received in my life–I think it would have been enough, but I have been fortunate to receive so much more. My entire family and I are very, very grateful for our experience in the game. I hope you get to enjoy the Game as much as I have–for, what amounts to, my whole life. Keep working hard.

Best of Luck,

Dick

Dick Corrigan
University of Maryland
Turnbull Award 1958

P.S. I am not sure that you will be getting a letter on behalf of the 1950 Turnbull Award recipient, Oliver "Corky" Shepard from Johns Hopkins, since he died a few years ago (perhaps Coach Scott has connected with his family), but I wanted to share a point that I think is worth passing along. Corky was selected for the South team in the 1950 North-South All-Star Game–a very prestigious and coveted honor. Corky declined the invitation and insisted that it go to one of his teammates who he felt was more deserving that season. I know of few people who would be so magnanimous. I hope you hear from someone on his behalf.

Dear Robbie,

Coach Scott asked me to write a note to you about a Turnbull Award winner, Jerry Schmidt (1962), who is my best friend. This note to you is because you have the special stick of the Turnbull brothers. The depth of my friendship is best expressed by quoting Robert Louis Stevenson: "Of what shall a man be proud, if he is not proud of his friends?"

Jerry and I met when we both played for the University Club that won the National Open Championship. That friendship blossomed into Jerry becoming my best man. While Jerry was associate coach at Navy he engineered the only win against the University of Maryland during my tenure. Even with his endless awards, I remember him as the man who saved my professional and personal life by convincing one of his former players, who was a head of school, to hire an old coach who couldn't find a job.

Let me tell you about another remarkable person! Coach Schmidt was in the hospital recovering from a major surgery, uncertain about his future as his whole life had been playing and coaching lacrosse. Former Army and Maryland coach, Dick Edell, came into Jerry's room quickly changing Jerry's mindset with the sharing of past lacrosse stories. Jerry told me if anyone needed advice about life or lacrosse he recommended contacting Coach Edell.

Best Wishes and Kindest Regards,

Dick Szlasa

Dear Robbie,

Congratulations on receiving the Magic Lacrosse Stick! A stick that with each passing of the hands, has received the generous love and respect that all lacrosse sticks should receive. I know it will bring you great satisfaction and success in your lacrosse endeavors, as my stick has done for me. For it is the 'stick' that allows the great sport of lacrosse to be played. Without sticks, there is no game. A game that is full of great skill, heart, and passion.

For myself, a Canadian by birth, I have had the privilege of playing this great sport in Canada and the United States. From the lacrosse hotbed of Orangeville, down to Virginia where I was a three-time All-American at Roanoke College, I come from three generations of Masons. My great uncle, Jack "Curly" Mason, won 6 Mann Cups and is in the Canadian Lacrosse Hall of Fame. My father, Robb Mason, won 5 Presidents Cups and played for the Team Canada 1984 to win the Continental Cup, and my sister, Paige Mason (Roanoke '10), played for Team Canada in 2007. I was also able to play with great teammates who enjoy the game as much as I do. These teammates taught me about hard work and winning, but most importantly, about respecting the game. If it wasn't for my teammates, coaches, and parents, I would have never won the Turnbull Award in 2007!

Robbie, as important as it is to learn from your coaches, I encourage you to always learn from your teammates. From the player with the most points, to the player with the most ground balls, everyone can contribute to your success. Every player is important in their own way to the team. Successful teams find ways to bring all of these skills together.

A book that you might like is *American Indian Lacrosse: Little Brother of War* by Dr. Tom Vennum!

As a college player, I finished my career with just under 250 goals. One piece of advice–every time you shoot on the goal, think net!

Yours in Lacrosse,

Jon Mason

Roanoke College, Lt. Col. John I. "Jack" Turnbull Award 2007

Robbie,

I grew up in Canada playing hockey and "box" lacrosse in the very rural town of St. David's in Southern Ontario! I used a wooden stick until I attended Cornell University as a freshman in 1973. The adjustment was difficult at first but I received a tremendous amount of help and support from my coaches and teammates. As a team in 1976, we (Cornell) won the National Championship in an overtime victory over the University of Maryland. We finished the season undefeated.

I am now 61 years of age and many of my closest friends in life shared that tremendous moment with me on the field that glorious day at Brown University. Great memories. My Cornell experience changed my life and I am and will continue to be eternally grateful.

The sport of lacrosse has done so much for me, my family, and so many of my friends and it can do the same for YOU! Enjoy the competition, respect your opponents and most of all cherish you teammates—they will become your lifelong best friends. Robbie, honor this great game and the relationships it will bring to you and I will guarantee you that the game will reward you in kind.

It's also interesting that you would be at Coach Bob Scott's home in Baltimore. I wholeheartedly agree with Coach Scott that the "old school" letter writing makes correspondence much more meaningful. I can say from first-hand experience...I received a wonderful note from Coach Scott, which I've saved to this day. I received this special note 38 years ago. I have very much cherished its contents so I thought it would be appropriate to share with you (attached).

The world of lacrosse is filled with so many special people...heroes who fought for our country like Lieutenant Colonel Jack Turnbull, and renowned National Championship coaches and role models like Bob Scott and my coach, mentor, and lifelong friend, Richie Moran.

Best wishes Robbie...follow your dreams and I hope our paths cross in the future.

Michael French

Cornell University 1976
Turnbull Award 1976
Team Canada 1974, 1978, and 1982
Canadian Lacrosse Hall of Fame, 2001
National Lacrosse Hall of Fame, Class of 1991
National Lacrosse League Hall of Fame, 2007

Dear Mike,

Congratulations for such a tremendous lacrosse season. I saw both Hopkins games and the big one with Maryland and there is no doubt you were the best player in the country in 1976. I know the committee that selected you as the recipient of the Enners Award had the easiest job in many years. You were the obvious winner.

What makes everyone who knows the game so happy is the fact that you represent all of the fine qualities of a truly great athlete. Your ways off the field are as exemplary as your performance on the field. Every coach I have spoken with about you has had nothing but good things to say about you.

I personally appreciated your speaking with me after the game in 1974 and it has been a real pleasure to watch you play from the stands last year and this year. You received help from Eamon and Jon, as well as your mid-fielders, but you were the key man. I am especially happy for you because you really deserve all of the honors you have received. And the beauty of it is–you will take them in stride.

Best of luck to you in your future endeavors– there's no doubt you will be most successful.

I will look forward to seeing you in the near future.

Sincerely,

Bob Scott

Dear Robbie,

I was fortunate to be part on some of the greatest Hobart College Lacrosse Teams that ever played the game. I accepted the Turnbull Award for the Division II-III Attackman of the Year in 1978 on behalf of my teammates. Lacrosse is a team sport, and your personal success rests on the hard work of all of your teammates, no matter their playing time. Rarely was a game as physical or intense as our daily Hobart practices.

Ironically, I write this to you after losing a close friend and teammate last week. Rick Blick was our All-American goalie. He defined hard work and dedication. He was the best! Rick outworked everyone in the game when he played.

Rick's exceptional work ethic forty years ago is the same work ethic that the "great ones" commit to today. Fads come and go. Things like hairstyles, clothing, technology, and music are always changing. However, the formula for success never changes. Characteristics like commitment, dedication, hard work, sacrifice, unselfishness, and loyalty still produce success for today's great athletes as it has throughout history.

I wish you the best of luck and would encourage you to read the book *Outliers* by Malcolm Gladwell. Gladwell discusses what makes high achievers different.

Robbie, enjoy the game and cherish the friends you will meet and make along the way. They will always live in your heart.

Best wishes,

Terry Corcoran

Wabash College Lacrosse Coach
Hobart College 1978
Turnbull Award 1978

Dear Robbie,

I write to you on behalf of the late Turnbull Award recipient Hezzy Howard and his family. I had the good fortune to play lacrosse at Washington College, coach there, and I am now the Director of Athletics, so I feel that I have a good sense of the College and the lacrosse program (I also had the good fortune to be the head lacrosse coach at the United States Naval Academy for twelve years). Hezzy was a major lacrosse star at Washington College in the 1950's, and in fact was a national star.

I had the opportunity to meet Hezzy and to get to know him, and he was a fantastic person. Most people may not know it, but Hezzy was the lacrosse coach and a brilliant English professor at the University of Maryland. He had a long and distinguished career there. From what I could gather from his former teammates, Hezzy was primarily a feeding attackman, who had great vision of the field and was totally unselfish.

I think Hezzy would have told you to enjoy yourself when you play, to remember it's a game, and to work as hard at your academics as you do at lacrosse. It will carry you far.

His family would recommend that you read *Carry On, Mr. Bowditch,* the Newberry Award book for the year Hezzy received the Turnbull Award—1956. It is interesting that the theme of the book is navigation—a subject that all of my players at Navy are intimately (sometimes more intimately than they wanted) familiar with! I hope you will enjoy reading it—particularly the part about "sailing by ash breeze."

My very best,

Bryan Matthews

Dear Robbie,

Hello, I am Brian Scheetz, the 2012 Turnbull Award recipient from Mercyhurst University. I hope you have been enjoying lacrosse as much as I have throughout my career. Lacrosse has taught me a lot in life and has helped me grow into the person I am today. I have been truly fortunate in the game, Robbie. I won a New York State high school state championship in 2009 during my senior year at Canandaigua Academy, as well as a National Championship at M&T Bank stadium in Baltimore, Maryland to conclude my sophomore campaign in 2011! The people I have met through the game of lacrosse have been a major part of my life and will continue to be a focal point in the future. The lacrosse community is very small but has rapidly shown growth across the nation. My lacrosse experience has been unbelievable and I would have never met the people I have without lacrosse in my life. I am currently attempting to give back to the game by coaching at Coker College in South Carolina.

Lacrosse is a team game but when you are recognized for your efforts individually, it is special. Receiving this award as a junior showed that all the work I had put in to the game over the years had paid off. This award would not have been possible without being on a successful team and so I have to thank my teammates for all of the work they put in as well. It truly means a lot to be recognized. Lacrosse has been on this earth for hundreds of years and is growing into one of the fastest growing sports across the nation. Jack is a legend of the game and will be remembered in the lacrosse community forever.

Coach Scott asked us to provide a couple of recommendations to you. First and foremost, I would say don't let anything hold you back from your dreams. Set goals and work hard every day to achieve those goals and do not let anyone deter you. The game of lacrosse can do a lot for you in life; you just have to put in what you want to get out of it. Learning the game of lacrosse is just as important as playing it. A player who understands the game and its situations is a valuable asset to any team. Play fast, play hard. Use the ground on shots. And make sure you are having fun while you play because when it becomes a job it is not a game. I am 5'5." I have always been told in sports that I was too small, not big enough, and not fast enough to be great. That is what drove me to work every day and keep a chip on my shoulder. People and coaches need to look more into player's heart and what they have inside of them. Attitude and passion for the game is irreplaceable and that is what winners have inside.

Also—take advantage of the opportunities God gives you, no matter the situation, find the good and do what you can to help others. Dream big and take chances because every day that goes by, you will never get that opportunity back to improve.

I would recommend that you read *Mind Gym: An Athlete's Guide to Inner Excellence* by Gary Mack and David Casstevens.

All the best, Robbie,

Brian Scheetz

Mercyhurst University 2013
Turnbull Award 2012

Dear Robbie,

I am so glad to hear of our connection to Jack Turnbull through your fantastic stick.

Lacrosse has been a huge part of my life for 35 years now. I played at John Jay-Cross River High School in South Salem, NY and then at Nazareth College. I am currently the head coach at Roger Williams University in Bristol, Rhode Island and have been for thirteen years. As great as lacrosse has been for me and meant to me—being the father of five children is even more meaningful.

By far, lacrosse has shaped who I am and what I have become. I still have tremendous friends and memories to this day from my time playing lacrosse; from high school thru college and even now; playing in an over-40 men's league.

I was fortunate to be a part of a championship team at Nazareth. I can't say why I was selected to receive the Turnbull Award but I like to think that I played a balanced game, ending my career with almost the same amount of goals and assists certainly helped. I always felt I played well within a team environment and could help dictate the play and tempo of our offense without being an overly athletic or flashy player.

A few thoughts that I may offer—be fundamentally sound! Throw, pass and catch the ball correctly and pick up ground balls. Having solid fundamentals allowed me to be a strong player. Also, worry about the team and the individual awards will come. Usually no one is honored with awards unless the team is successful. Individual awards are terrific, however winning as a team is always remembered more than the individual accomplishments. I would also say that everything in life happens for a reason. The harder you work the luckier you will seem to be.

I'm not sure that I fully appreciated the magnitude of receiving the Lt. Col. J. I. "Jack" Turnbull Award, but I can assure you that twenty years later I fully realize how fortunate I am to have received such an honor while playing a truly magnificent game. Having learned more about the life of Jack Turnbull has only magnified my pride in receiving this Award. In his short life, he sacrificed and accomplished more than most humans ever will and as I continue to get older, my pride and honor will only grow greater. I am proud to have my name associated with you and Jack Turnbull!

I wish you all the best in your playing and academic careers, Robbie. I am sure that you will conduct your life in a manner that would make Col. Turnbull proud. Please let me know if there is anything I can do to help you!

I would recommend that you read the book *Tuesdays With Morrie* by Mitch Albom.

Sincerely,

Marty Kelly

Head Lacrosse Coach
Roger Williams University
Lt. Col. John I. "Jack" Turnbull Award 1992
Nazareth College 1992

Dear Robbie,

Congratulations on receiving the special lacrosse stick from CAPT Lewis! I received the Turnbull Award at Cortland State University in 2008. Being the recipient of the Turnbull Award was a great honor for me but it was all based on having a great team and unselfish play on offense.

Lacrosse has been a very special part of my life. Lacrosse is a great game for a competitive young athlete with unlimited opportunity to move onto college. It can not only open doors to a desired school, but also teaches values that are used in the work world. Work ethic developed in lacrosse translates directly into success in the business world. I would encourage you to enjoy every minute of playing competitive lacrosse and grow and develop every day as an athlete and person. Putting in the extra work off the field is what will allow a young athlete to become the best player they can be.

My lacrosse experience at Cortland State University was great. We developed a work ethic and brotherhood that translated to success on the field and friendship off. We won the national championship vs. Salisbury in an incredible OT game, which was the best experience of my life. The next two years playing in the national championship were memorable as well even though we lost both years. The lessons learned from a loss are carried onto the rest of your life and can be used in a positive way to always strive for success and to be the best at what you do.

I think I was selected for the Turnbull Award for my leadership and work ethic. I have always been a team player that would rather draw a double and hit a cutter on the back door for a lay-up than getting a shot myself and scoring. This leads to a more unselfish overall offense and a fluid team concept.

I have coached numerous youth teams and lacrosse camps and still enjoy teaching young players the game, how to be a team player, and what they need to do on and off the field to be successful.

Coach Beville's philosophy was always hard work and doing the extra off the field to get an edge on the competition. Lifting weights, running stadiums, and playing wall ball is the quickest way to get an edge on other teams.

I did not having the speed and strength coming out of high school to compete at the level I wanted. Consistent weight training, running stadiums, and healthy eating led to a level of fitness that let me achieve all the goals that I set in my college career from three-time All-American, to Attackman of the Year, and, mostly, national champion.

It is an honor to be connected to you through Jack Turnbull. Best of luck!

All the best,

Ryan Heath

Turnbull Award 2008
Cortland State University 2008

Dear Robbie,

I write to you on behalf of Bob Scott in regard to your special stick. Let me begin by saying that I have considered Coach Scott a mentor for all these years. He and my coach, Henry Ciccarone,–both great men and great coaches–have meant a great deal to me and countless other young men. I feel very fortunate to have had great relationships with both of these legends.

I grew up in a town called Massapequa on the South Shore of Long Island. I live in Breckenridge, Colorado now and have for many years. I played at Massapequa High School and then at Johns Hopkins University in Baltimore and ultimately for the USA Team in 1982. I was fortunate to win a county championship at Massapequa, then a national championship at Johns Hopkins and, yes, a world championship with Team USA! I can tell you that I enjoyed the journey at every step–never really focusing on the championships themselves, but the work and preparation that went into trying to do my best.

I received the Turnbull Award in 1977 and 1978. I think at the time I was very gratified to receive it and now–when I think back–it is a very nice memory of playing with and against some truly great players and teams.

If I could give you some advice on how to succeed–it might be to bring good energy to the field and locker room. I tried very hard to do that every day. Also–be aggressive, have fun with the game, work hard, play hard and remember that it is a game. I think if you keep a good attitude and work hard, good things will happen for you.

My coaches (Pat Oleksiak at MHS and "Chic" at JHU) stressed the fundamentals–and to push the ball all the time. We scrimmaged in every practice and genuinely had fun competing.

Lacrosse has provided me with great relationships with my teammates and coaches, as well as the people I have met due to my playing the game, and allowed me travel opportunities around the world. I have been lucky enough to play lacrosse in Australia, San Francisco, Dallas, Florida, North Carolina, New York, etc.

Coach Scott asked me to include a recommendation for a book–and I heartily commend *The Prince* by Niccolò Machiavelli to you!

I hope that you enjoy playing the game as much as I have and that it will continue to be a central part of your life–like it has for me. Keep working hard and best of luck with your stick.

Yours in Lacrosse,

Michael O'Neill

Johns Hopkins University 1978
Turnbull Award 1977, 1978
Team USA 1982
National Lacrosse Hall of Fame, Class of 1993

[RHS Note: I did not get to coach Mike, but served as Athletic Director during his time at Hopkins.]

Dear Robbie,

I understand that we are connected through your association with a special lacrosse stick once held by Jack Turnbull. My connection to Jack is that I was fortunate to receive the Award named after him three times while I was playing at Salisbury University. Great to "meet" you!

Lacrosse was one of the greatest things to come into my life. Before 8th grade, I didn't even know what the sport was. But I found out at Carthage High School (where I still coach) it was a game that combined "goal scoring" from so many other sports with the contact of football. It was perfect for me. Lacrosse has allowed me to go compete at the college level, be a part of two national championship teams, get several individual accolades, travel all over the country doing clinics and camps, and helped me become who I am today.

Receiving the award was a great honor. Receiving it the second and then third time was even more special. I believe I received the award because I played on great teams and was fortunate enough to lead them in points. Jack's is a truly inspirational story. He was a complete student and unbelievable athlete and a great leader and American who was dedicated to his country.

If I could pass along a little advice, I would say that it doesn't matter what your shape or size is. If you work harder than the other guy, you have a chance. If you take a chance you never know where you might end up. Anything is possible if you believe it is.

Make sure you play every minute as if it is your last. You never know when your playing days may come to an end. Make sure you tell the people you love most that you love them EVERY chance you can. When they are gone you will probably wish you could tell them every day.

I can't thank my coaches enough. My high school coach, Kirk Ventiquattro, taught us to work hard to learn the game. He really made you want to work to be the best. My college coach, Jim Berkman, refined my skills and pushed me to dominate. He made me realize that if you worked on your skills and put yourself in a position to be great you were cheating yourself if you didn't play great. He made me be the best every day.

I have several memories, but the moments I remember best are (1) my first day of fall practice in college my freshman year. I got the ball knocked away from me and beaten up every time I touched the ball. It motivated me to get better FAST! (2) First day of practice in 8th grade. NO IDEA what was going on or what to expect. (3) 1994 National

Championship–Salisbury's first. (4) 1995 road trips with the team. We were a complete team and we all got along great. We played–and won–as a TEAM.

When I was a freshman in college I was 5'8 and 215 pounds. I was not very fast either. People always looked at me like I couldn't do "it." I was too small and slow to get any job done on the field. I had to prove myself every step of the way.

Looking back, lacrosse has meant so much to me. To receive an Award named after someone who was such a complete student, athlete and American is quite an honor indeed. I hope you'll enjoy your relationship with Jack Turnbull and the game as much as I have.

A book I would recommend is *Bleachers* by John Grisham.

Good luck with the stick and your playing career.

All the Best,

Jason Coffman

Carthage High School 1992
Salisbury University 1995
Turnbull Award 1993, 1994, 1995

Dear Robbie,

Congratulations on being selected by Captain Lewis to receive the magical lacrosse stick. That is quite an accomplishment and you should be very proud. I was humbled when Coach Scott requested that I reach out to you regarding the Turnbull Award and my experiences with the game that has given me so much. Using my experiences, I will do my best to give you some advice that you might be able to use one day.

My name is Steele Stanwick, and I was fortunate enough to receive the Turnbull Award in the spring of 2012 at the University of Virginia. I grew up in Baltimore, Maryland and come from a large family (I am 1 of 8), where we all played lacrosse through college. Lacrosse has always been an important part of my life and family. Undoubtedly, one of the primary reasons I am so grateful for the sport of lacrosse is because it always brought my family closer together, and is a passion we can always share; and for that I am very thankful.

After attending Loyola Blakefield High School, I was fortunate enough to attend the University of Virginia. Fast-forward 4 years, I was receiving the Turnbull Award my senior year and I could not have been more humbled and honored. Just to be mentioned in the same breath as Jack Turnbull is one of the greatest compliments I've ever received. One of the reasons receiving the Jack Turnbull Award is so gratifying is because I have so much respect for the game, the award, and for Jack Turnbull himself. While that depth of respect may be rare in many sports, it is common in the lacrosse world.

Robbie, if I could give you any advice it would be to respect the game of lacrosse in all aspects, enjoy the game, and work/practice so hard so that win, lose, or draw you can look in the mirror and be happy with yourself.

Respect the people that have played before you and respect the ones that will play after you. The relationships and opportunities that I have made playing lacrosse are amazing. Lacrosse is such a special sport in so many ways. It will give you so much if you treat it the right away. This is, in part, due to the fact that the lacrosse community is such a close-knit group where there is so much respect for everyone; it is what separates lacrosse from the rest.

In short, I was able to use a game that I loved playing to achieve my dreams. I was fortunate enough to win a National Championship and the Tewaaraton Award, attend my dream school, and more importantly, build relationships that will last forever. All of this I believe stemmed from the fact that I respected the game first.

My college coach, Dom Starsia, would always remind his players to "enjoy the journey." And I encourage you to do the same thing. Enjoy every part of your lacrosse experience. Enjoy the tough practices, runs, lifts, bus rides, team movies, road trips…That's the good stuff.

All of these opportunities would not have been possible if I was not blessed with the ability to play lacrosse. I attribute a lot of my success to the fact that I was blessed with certain talents, but also to the fact that I work very hard and spend a tremendous amount of time practicing. Malcom Gladwell wrote a book called *Outliers.* In the book he talks about how if you want to be successful at anything in life, you have to dedicate about 10,000 hours to practice. I promise that with 10,000 hours of practice with your magical lacrosse stick, you will be writing one of these letters one day.

Very truly yours,

Steele Stanwick

University of Virginia
Lt. Col. John I. "Jack" Turnbull Award 2012

Dear Robbie,

I have been in recent contact with Coach Scott in regard to you being in possession of the special lacrosse stick once used by the famous Turnbull brothers. My late father, Don Hahn, received the Turnbull Award in 1951 as a player at Princeton University.

My father was once described by John Steadman of *The Sunday American and the News-Post* as "the greatest lacrosser to turn a stick in his palms since the late, lamented Jack Turnbull." Apparently their similarities did not stop with success on the lacrosse field. Steadman also wrote that both were "quiet, reserved, and gentlemanly."

A child named Jack Turnbull (the nephew of the Award's namesake) presented the Turnbull Award to Don in 1951. While details of that day may be lost to history, my father did recall telling the young fellow, "I did not know the man for whom you are named, but I understand that he is considered the greatest lacrosse player ever."

Don received a number of awards during his career in addition to the Turnbull Award. He received Princeton's top lacrosse award, the Higginbotham Trophy, in 1950 and 1951, and was a two-time First-Team All-America selection in those same years. In 1981, Don was elected into the National Lacrosse Hall of Fame.

My father's enjoyment of the game and respect for its traditions were obvious in speeches he made, though he seldom spoke of his own accomplishments, such was his modesty. Upon Don's induction into the Hall of Fame, a teammate, Frank "Skip" Eccles wrote, "It is a particular pleasure to see the honor going to someone who bore his considerable success with such modesty and who always struck me as a most admirable person in every way."

Speaking at the United States Intercollegiate Lacrosse Association (USILA) December dinner meeting in New York honoring the All-America Team of 1950, my father remarked,

"...We also have a great sense of responsibility—a responsibility to all of you gentlemen assembled here this evening in the common interest of lacrosse, a responsibility to the game itself. Looking back at the imposing list of those who were once honored as we are tonight and who have done so much, through example if not actual participation, to maintain the high caliber of intercollegiate lacrosse throughout the years, we can find much inspiration for meeting this responsibility.

"And so we accept this challenge of preserving in lacrosse what we consider vital to it. Chief among these is the high standard of competition balanced by an amazing degree of good will and congeniality among the competitors....Win or lose–it has always been fun to play lacrosse–and a privilege too. We shall do our best to preserve these fundamental elements of the game."

Some 30 years later, Don would make the following remarks on the occasion of his induction into the Hall of Fame in 1982 at Homewood Field, Baltimore:

"For myself with humility and thanks; for my family with pride; with gratitude to my schools and coaches; with a bow to the fine competitors I have played against; and in recognition of–and ultimately on behalf of–those wonderful people and players–my teammates, without whom obviously this Award would never have come to me.

"With all of these feelings, I accept this honor today from my former coaches and can only wish for those playing now or yet to come, that the beautiful game of lacrosse continues to provide the experience of clean sport and lasting friendships–among opponents as well as teammates–and *just plain fun* that it was my good fortune to know."

These words, spoken by my father over the last half a century, still ring true today. I hope, as my father would, that you find clean sport, lasting friendships, and of course, just plain fun!

Best of luck,

Tobin Hahn

In memory of Donald Hahn
Turnbull Award 1951
All-America Team 1950, 1951
Higginbotham Trophy 1950, 1951
National Championship, Princeton 1951
National Lacrosse Hall of Fame, Class of 1981

Dear Robbie,

I am excited for you to embark on this journey. As you travel down your respective path, I am sure you will hear that lacrosse is more than just a game. It is not all about winning and losing but about teamwork, friendship, sportsmanship and becoming a leader. Lacrosse has the ability to shape your life as it did mine.

My name is David Maguire and I grew up just outside of Philadelphia in Broomall, Pennsylvania. As I reflect back on my childhood, all I can remember is wanting to play soccer and baseball. That was until I was introduced to lacrosse at twelve years old. From that day on I was hooked. All I wanted to do was play in the backyard and throw the ball against the small brick wall next to my driveway. After hours and hours of wall ball and countless broken windows (Oops…sorry Mom & Dad), my parents made a goal for me to shoot on. This is where all of the hard work started to pay off and my lacrosse skills were born.

My high school coach was Tom Hannum. He taught me to work toward my goals, play hard and never give up. His positive attitude made lacrosse fun. Coach Hannum always had my back. Win or lose it was about making yourself better every day. He was the one that cemented my love for the game and gave me the drive to play at my best always.

I played collegiate lacrosse at Ohio Wesleyan University (OWU) and was a three-time First-Team All-American just like Lieutenant Colonel Jack Turnbull. I was fortunate to be coached by John Zulberti (Jack Turnbull Award recipient 1988 & 1989). John taught us how to play the game two steps ahead and make the right play not just the next one. In 1997 my junior year I was the recipient of the Jack Turnbull Award. This was one of the most significant moments of my career. The following season in 1998, my senior year, my teammate and close friend Darren McGurn was received the Jack Turnbull Award. For me, the fact that my coach and good friend were both awarded the Jack Turnbull award was very special and meaningful. It played an important part in shaping my life and who I am today.

Lacrosse has provided so many opportunities to me over the years; I have traveled the world, met many outstanding people, and learned how to be a leader. As I reflect back on the success I had in my career one thing I will never forget is the true mark of a champion is what you do when others aren't looking. Lacrosse will open many doors for you Robbie, but it is up to you to make the best of it.

All the best to you,

David Maguire

Ohio Wesleyan University 1998
Turnbull Award Recipient 1997
Ohio Wesleyan University Hall of Fame 2009

Centennial High School
History Department

Dear Robbie,

It is a great honor to have the opportunity to participate in your magical journey through lacrosse history. As I'm sure you have become aware, lacrosse is a game whose greatness lies not only in the excitement and beauty of its play, but even more in the nature of the people that play and support the game.

I have been fortunate to benefit from those great people. In looking back at my career, I can proudly list a number of honors that have come my way. We won a national championship with Hopkins in 1974 and a World Championship that same year. I played on two undefeated teams at Towson High School under the leadership of my father, Bill Thomas. I also was selected for some individual awards during those years. Those accomplishments, however, fade into the background, and what is remembered are the great people with whom I shared those experiences. My heroes, like Captain Lewis, my coaches, like Coach Scott, and my teammates are what I hold on to. They are the real beauty of the game.

As you go forward, work hard, strive for success, enjoy the playing, but most importantly enjoy the lifelong relationships that come with playing lacrosse.

Good Luck.

Jack Thomas

Johns Hopkins University 1974
Turnbull Award 1973, 1974
Team USA 1974
National Lacrosse Hall of Fame, Class of 1989

Dear Robbie,

What an honor it is to write a note on behalf of the Turnbull Award and the significance it carries in the game of lacrosse–past, present and forever. My name is Roy McAdam, a proud recipient of this award while playing at Hobart College in 1980. I am honored to be associated with this award that showcases the greatest scorers in the history of the game.

Back at age 13, I bought my first wooden box lacrosse stick from an Indian reservation in Canada called Cornwall. That stick brought me an immediate connection to the game and to the fundamentals of learning how to pass and catch. I used to spend hours a day hitting the ball against walls and playing catch with friends and family. It was at that point in my life that I realized lacrosse was not just a sport to me, it was a passion.

I played high school at a small school in upstate NY named General Brown under Coach Steve Fisher and Coach Jim Branski. Our team was always an underdog because our stick skills were limited compared to other teams in the Syracuse area. But our coaches taught us toughness and perseverance. At Hobart, I was no longer playing on an underdog team. Our players still possessed limited stick skills compared to other teams in the Long Island and Baltimore areas, but like my high school team, we brought a physical presence to the game that intimidated opponents. Playing at these levels taught me how to play the game of lacrosse physically and fearlessly.

Playing lacrosse at a high level and in "big" games was both exciting and fun, but the best experience was sharing those moments with my family. My passion for lacrosse was my family's passion and my family's passion was mine. My biggest fans were my parents, Bruce and Doris, and my brothers, Bruce Jr. and Fred. But my biggest fan of all was my sister, Beth Bauer. I love you all and thank you for your support.

Lacrosse is in many ways like life. We experience many highs and lows and we learn from those experiences. The biggest lesson I've learned playing lacrosse was from my late Coach Jerry Schmidt. I was given a starting attackman position my sophomore year and was having a rough go at it. My confidence was at its lowest going up against the long defensive sticks and I even told the coach that there were better players on the bench. Coach reinforced me that I had more talent than those on the bench and even designed plays around me to build my confidence. That was a pivotal point in my lacrosse career. I went on to become MVP of the

NCAA Tournament that year and, ultimately, reached the highest of the highs in team and individual awards in my career.

Great players come out of great programs. No one deserves more credit to building Hobart into a lacrosse powerhouse than the legendary "Babe" Krause. The leadership continued during my tenure from Athletic Director Bill Stiles and Chief Financial Officer William Van Arsdale. It continues to this day with the current Athletic Director, Mike Hanna, at the helm. I was very thankful and honored to have played for two legendary coaches, Jerry Schmidt and Dave Urick. They have been great teachers in lacrosse and life to me and to so many. And those many include great teammates such as Dave McNaney, Terry Corcoran, Tom Schardt, the late Rick Blick, Jim Calder and Marc Darcangelo. In the end of my career, I was the beneficiary of three national championships (1976, 1977, and 1980). I am indebted to Hobart College Lacrosse Program for that honor and for the honor of receiving the Turnbull Award my senior year. I wish you all the best!

With great joy and pride,

Roy McAdam

Hobart College 1980
Turnbull Award and Player of the Year 1980
Hobart Hall of Fame, Class of 2014

Hi Robbie,

I am very glad to connect with you concerning my Turnbull Award in 1979. I grew up in Levittown, New York and played at Levittown Division High School and then at the University of Maryland. My lacrosse experience was fun, exciting, and I made life-long friends all over the world.

I would recommend that you work hard every day in practice, enjoy the game, and remember that lacrosse is a team sport–not an individual sport. Let lacrosse guide your life not run your life. At Maryland we had a little mantra we called "Be the Best" which meant to give your all all the time.

Receiving the Turnbull Award was very special for me. It was presented to me at a dinner before the North-South game–I felt so proud to receive it in front of my peers. I know that Jack was a tremendous player, athlete, and person, and that he died in the service of our country. I made a very brief speech when I accepted the Award and I think I said what a great honor it was to receive an award named after such a great man and how proud I was to be associated with him. I am equally proud to now be associated with you. I never could have imagined back then what this Award would mean to me thirty-five years later!

I hope that you–and as many young players as possible–will get the opportunity to continue to play lacrosse and experience the fun that I did and be a part of the lacrosse family that comes with playing the game.

A book that I would recommend you read is *A Short Guide to a Happy Life* by Anna Quindlen.

Best of Luck.

Bob Boneillo

University of Maryland
Turnbull Award 1979

Dear Robbie,

Greetings from Jack Daut, Turnbull Award recipient at Rutgers University in 1957!

I am honored to share some remembrances about the Turnbull Award from so many years ago. Briefly, I played my high school ball at Sewanhaka High School in Floral Park, Long Island for the legendary coach, Bill Ritch. I then played at Rutgers University for Al Twitchell. Receiving the Turnbull Award was a great honor but totally unexpected. I remember that when I was told I was to receive the Award I was totally flabbergasted!

I learned early in my career (at Sewanhaka) to catch the ball and quickly release it. I became known for my "quick stick." I think this skill, along with my quick feet helped me score many goals and assists. In 1957, Jim Brown–the great football and lacrosse All-American from Syracuse University–and I tied for the national scoring honors with forty-something goals. That year, one of my fond memories was receiving a wonderful complement from a Mount Washington (one of, if not *the*, best teams in the country at the time) defenseman after our game.

I'd say that lacrosse is a great game, with lots of action and challenge. It requires athleticism, skill, speed, intuitive abilities, and, above all, unselfish teamwork. Learn the fundamentals of the game and practice them religiously! My coaches used to preach fundamentals, fundamentals, fundamentals, as well as staying in shape, staying positive and practicing. No surprises there, I suspect.

I hope my words here will be of some use to you. I have been attempting to repay the kindness and support of Coach Ritch for my whole life. He was a great coach who took a sincere interest in each of his players and their lives. He taught me the fundamentals of the game and was instrumental in my being able to go to college. In my senior year he lined up full scholarships to Rutgers, Syracuse, and West Point. Lacrosse and Bill Ritch were truly a turning point in my life!

As you move through your life, I would recommend that you work hard, stay focused, persevere in doing your best, and don't let adversity detour you from your goals.

A book I might recommend to you would be *David and Goliath David: Underdogs, Misfits, and the Art of Battling Giants* by Malcolm Gladwell.

My very best wishes.

Jack Daut

Rutgers University 1957
Turnbull Award 1957

Robbie,

Great to connect with you. I am DJ Hessler from Tufts University and Turnbull recipient in 2011. I have had a lacrosse stick in my hand since the moment I could crawl. It started with soft-stick clinics and continues to this day. It is a game that I have and will always continue to love and cannot wait to pass down to the next generation. I grew up in Baltimore County, playing recreational and travel league until I enrolled at St. Paul's School for Boys and began playing for the Crusaders. My first two years in high school I played on the JV team. I made varsity my junior year but only saw time on Man-up situations. Unfortunately, with the way recruiting was, and how each year younger and younger kids are committing, not playing substantially until your senior year does not afford you many options. I was interested in several Division I schools, but ultimately decided to go to Tufts University where they had an on-the-rise program and a great engineering school.

The greatest of my lacrosse experiences was winning the 2010 Division III national championship over Salisbury. I would have traded any award I earned my senior year (2011), when we lost in a rematch against Salisbury, to have won another championship. After my senior year I was drafted by the Boston Cannons of Major League Lacrosse in the post-collegiate waiver draft and practiced with them on several occasions during the 2011 and 2012 seasons but was ultimately waived. I still continue to play in local indoor and outdoor leagues, and don't ever imagine myself stopping.

Receiving the Turnbull Award was obviously quite an honor for me. However, individual awards have never been as important to me as winning, because awards represent for the most part a judgment or an opinion. The Award would have meant nothing to me if our team was not successful. That being said, receiving the Turnbull Award was a great accomplishment and honor. It was a goal of mine at the beginning of the season to be the best attackman in the nation, so it was very satisfying to fulfill that individual goal.

I think to be a great attackman, you need to be a complete player, with an understanding of your offensive role, but also how the defense works and reacts. I have always thought of myself as a skilled feeder with excellent field vision, but as I aged, I became more of a threat to take it to the cage. Additionally, playing the "X" position is most similar in my mind to that of quarterback or point guard. Not only are you largely responsible for controlling the tempo of your offense, but you are also responsible for initializing and dictating the matchups. It requires not only physical talent and skill, but the mental aptitude to know what is best for your team in any given situation. I have always tried to be a cerebral player, and for my earlier career that carried me as my physical development occurred later on.

Some advice I would offer to become a complete threat is to not limit yourself early. Do not be afraid to make mistakes when you are trying something new, even if it is initially awkward or uncomfortable. Try new positions and play different sports, it keeps it all exciting and fresh. I really wish I could go back and tell my younger self to develop my off-hand until I felt equally comfortable with either hand. I feel completely confident in both hands, but I know there are certain things that I am not capable of doing with my off-hand that provide some limitations in what I do. By practicing (wallball, shooting, cradling) equally with both hands, you make yourself that much harder to predict and defend. Love the game and surround yourself with others who feel the same way. There is no better way to improve your game and to enjoy all the time you spend around it than by developing strong relationships with your teammates and friends and practicing together.

My coach used to say, "Make mistakes of commission not omission." Some would consider this a bit unorthodox approach, but with Coach Daly, it was always about attacking advantages and mismatches in transition. Having faith to dodge to the goal in unsettled and 5v5 situations created countless opportunities. Certainly, a fair amount of turnovers comes with pushing the ball, but by playing our up-tempo style, we were able to create many more high-percentage scoring chances than in settled 6v6 situations. Coach Daly was an unbelievable motivator and leader. Everyone on the team bought into his program and, as such, each individual was compelled to put in the work so as not to let down Coach, but more importantly not to let our teammates down. Whether it was a starter or a practice squad player, every person was accountable.

I have had countless memorable moments in my career–the national championship is definitely at the top. But in terms of meaningful events I have to tell you about the time we spent together on team community service projects. Each year we helped out at Cradles for Crayons where we worked to sort and prepare packages, such as gifts or clothes, for local needy children. Not only were these events unbelievably rewarding, but also the amount of team bonding that occurred is simply unmatched.

Most of all it was such a humbling experience and further reiterates how lucky many of us have it.

I have had to battle through a number of difficulties during my career—but everything has been more than worth it. I hope you will find your experience to be as rewarding as I have mine. Keep working hard. You are almost certain to have to fight through some difficulties—injuries, losses, etc. But if you stay focused on improving every day, I think you'll end up where you should.

A book that you may enjoy is *Lacrosse: Technique and Tradition, 2nd Edition*, Coach Dave Pietramala's updated edition of the Bob Scott classic.

Best of luck, Robbie,

DJ Hessler

Tufts University 2012
Turnbull Award 2011

Dear Robbie,

Please allow me to introduce myself. I am Ray Altman, Turnbull Award recipient at the University of Maryland in 1963. I am glad to share some thoughts with you at the request of Bob Scott.

Lacrosse was an integral part of my high school and college experience and provided an aspect of character building that cannot be taught or learned in the classroom. It was a tremendous honor for me to receive the Award, but I have never considered it to be mine alone– but a recognition that belonged to my entire team and coaches. I still feel that way today. My family actually accepted the Award for me because I was in New York at the North South game at the time of the presentation of the Award.

I recommend that you give your best to the game–consequently you will always be proud of your lacrosse experience. Enjoy the game, but get the best education possible, as it will pay dividends your entire life.

Lacrosse has been very good to me. I enjoyed every minute of my playing days and now have enjoyed many decades of great relationships with many people that I met through the game. I am certain that someday you'll feel the same way.

Ray Altman

Turnbull Award 1963
University of Maryland

[RHS Note: Ray sent me a copy of his Turnbull Award certificate, which I include here so that you can see the form it has taken over the years.]

PRESENTATION OF THE JACK TURNBULL TROPHY

Homewood Field, Baltimore, Maryland
June 7, 1963
Club All-Star Lacrosse Game

In memory of an all-time great lacrosse player, it is the privilege of the Mount Washington Lacrosse Club to award annually a trophy to the outstanding collegiate attack man to play on Maryland soil during the current season.

The Trophy is given in honor of Jack Turnbull, who gave his life in the service of our Country during World War II. Jack prepped at Poly; and, playing for Johns Hopkins, on this very field, became a first team All-American, an Olympian in 1932, and a member of the University's Hall of Fame of All-Time Greats. Jack Turnbull then continued his skillful play for nine years as a member of the Mount Washington Lacrosse Club. But Jack was much more than a highly talented lacrosse player. He was a perfect example of fine sportsmanship, an excellent team player, and a gentleman on and off the field.

The recipient of the Jack Turnbull Trophy is selected by all of the lacrosse coaches of Maryland college teams. Their choice of the outstanding attack man for the current season is Ray Altman of the University of Maryland. Ray prepped at City College where his prowess earned him All-Maryland honor, the Kelly Trophy as the outstanding prep lacrosse player, and the Fitzpatrick Award for sportsmanship. Ray Altman graduates this month from the University of Maryland. Last year he was second team All-American in lacrosse, and he has been named the Atlantic Coast Conference's outstanding athlete at the University. Criteria for this honor includes scholastic achievement. The Maryland coaches have chosen well, and on behalf of the Mount Washington Lacrosse Club, and I know I speak for the lacrosse community; I extend congratulations to Ray Altman, and Dr. Faber, his coach at the University.

The presentation tonight of the Jack Turnbull Trophy will be made by Mr. Douglas C. Turnbull, Jr., brother of the late Jack Turnbull. Doug also is an all-time great lacrosse player, elected to the Lacrosse Hall of Fame, and an outstanding alumnus of Johns Hopkins. Doug played for the Mount Washington Club for thirteen years and was our coach for two years.

Ray Altman tomorrow is participating in the North-South College All-Star game at Lake Placid, New York. He has asked his mother, Mrs. Louise H. Helman, to receive his award for him. Mrs. Helman, we appreciate your proudness of your son.

George C. O'Connell

President
Mount Washington Club, Inc.

Hi Robbie,

I am so glad to be asked to share some thoughts with you concerning the great game of lacrosse. I played at Yorktown High School and then Syracuse University. I have to tell you that I could not have been more fortunate in the game. I had truly great teammates and coaches all the way through and I will be forever grateful for my association with the game.

Beyond the national championship and personal awards (the Turnbull being my most cherished), what remains with me after all these years are my relationships in the game. I played for two great coaches–Gerry Walsh at Yorktown and Roy Simmons, Jr. (National Lacrosse Hall of Fame) at Syracuse–both of whom were great mentors to me. A number of my teammates are currently Hall of Fame members, as well. I also learned a great deal from a gentleman named Charlie Murphy (a Princeton graduate from the 1930s), who started lacrosse at Yorktown by purchasing the first two goals and who was the "Grandfather" of the program. "Mr. Murph," as he was referred to, was inducted into the Lacrosse Hall of Fame in 1998. I knew how much all of those people meant to me while I was playing–but they mean more and more to me with each passing year.

I've heard it said that a measure of a person it not what "belongs to us–but what we belong to." I belong to my family and teammates, to Yorktown High School, and Syracuse University. I could not want anything more than that.

I'd recommend that you spend as much time as you can with your stick–take it everywhere you go. You want it to be an extension of your body. Work on the wall. Change hands–you want to be as good as possible with each hand.

I have been truly blessed in the game and I hope you will enjoy your experience just a fraction as much as I have. Please let me know if I may be of any assistance to you in your journey.

A book you might enjoy is *InSideOut Coaching* by Joe Ehrmann (a fellow Syracuse alumnus!). I think you can learn quite a bit from Coach Ehrmann–and also from and about my coach at Syracuse, Roy Simmons, Jr.

All my best,

Tim Nelson

Syracuse University
Turnbull Award 1983, 1984, 1985
National Lacrosse Hall of Fame, Class of 2012

Hi Robbie,

What an honor to be invited to meet you by Coach Scott! I am very intrigued and interested to hear about your special stick. Perhaps we can meet in person and you can tell me about it sometime.

You know, Robbie, I don't even know where to start...lacrosse has been such a major part of my life for as long as I can remember. I am the youngest of three brothers. My older brothers, Bill (National Lacrosse Hall of Fame) and Tom, played before me at Massapequa High School and then Cornell University, where they racked up all sorts of awards and championships (too many to mention here). I tell you this because I could not have been more fortunate in my lacrosse "upbringing." Not only were my brothers true stars of the game–but I was fortunate to spend time with their teammates and coaches–true legends of the game. What a treat!

When I received the Turnbull Award in 1986–I was already familiar with it because my brothers' teammates had received it in prior years. To be in the same group as the likes of Mike O'Neill (Hopkins) and Mike French and Eamon McEananey (Cornell) (not to mention Jack himself), was very humbling to me and also a true honor.

As I look back on the game and think of some recommendations for you, I would start with the thought, "Be that guy!" Be that guy on your team who wants the ball at the end of the game. Be that guy in your business that people want to work with or for. Be that guy who gets things done when they need to get done. Also–anticipate and understand the game. Stay ahead of what is going on. What are you doing when you don't have the ball? Are you setting up a cut or shot? Anticipate what is next. I believe my anticipation of the game was developed form the countless High School, College and Club lacrosse games I watched of my older brothers.

I can't say enough about what my brothers, teammates, and coaches have meant to me all these years. I simply would not have achieved anything without their help. My coaches were great, coaches Adams, Long, and Arena at Virginia (two are in the Lacrosse Hall of Fame and the other [Arena] is in the Long Island Lacrosse and National *Soccer* Halls of Fame!). I owe a lot of my development and success to Coach Jeff Long and his arrival at UVA my junior year. He pushed me to succeed and to believe in my abilities as a player. My teammates are still among my very best friends. I had so, so many highlights but they all just wrap into a truly wonderful experience in the game.

Best of luck with your stick. Keep working on your skills and keep studying the game. I hope we get to connect soon.

Sincerely,

Roddy Marino

University of Virginia 1986
Turnbull Award 1986
Team USA 1986, 1990
National Lacrosse Hall of Fame, Class of 2002

Dear Robbie,

Mrs. Lee Hual, widow of the late Percy Williams, USNA '55, and Turnbull Award recipient that year, asked me to write to you in regard to Percy's lacrosse accomplishments, which brought back many positive memories. I joined the Navy team as a sophomore in the spring of 1955, Percy's senior year. I had known him in 1953 as we were in the same Company for a year when I was a freshman. He had talked to me numerous times when he found out I was playing on the freshman lacrosse team, and encouraged me from time to time during the season.

The Navy lacrosse team won the National Championship in 1954, so when I came out for the varsity in 1955, I knew that the competition would be tough at the attack position. Fortunately, I was left-handed and had an advantage of being able to more accurately pass the ball to my teammates at the midfield and attack position. Here again, Percy had made that point to me and worked out with me separately many times before and after regular practice. The result being that I became the starter at that position, opposite Percy, during the season.

The season went well for the team; we won the first six games handily with Percy racking up many goals each game. The seventh game was against our biggest rival, Maryland, and was essentially the game for another national championship. Unfortunately, we lost 9–8 in the last seconds of the game, but again, Percy led the offense for the team. His performance in that game sealed his position for selection as a First-Team All-American; and, more importantly, the winner of the Jack Turnbull Memorial Award presented to the nation's top attackman. Navy went on to win the remaining three games. Navy held all teams that year to single digits, while scoring double digits (up to 21 goals) in every game, primarily due to Percy's outstanding scoring capabilities.

For the remaining two years I played at Navy, there were many times I reflected on how Percy had mentored me through his patience, cajoling, and lighthearted personality. He was a winner in all respects, and I value his memories as a teammate and friend.

I hope that you'll be lucky enough to have a teammate like Percy at some point in your career. More importantly, I hope that you will *be* a teammate like Percy. It has meant the world to me all these years.

Good luck.

Shannon Heyward
Navy Lacrosse '57
[RHS Note: Shannon was a three-time All-American at Navy and is a retired Navy Captain!]

Robbie,

I hope you are enjoying your special stick. I hope the game of lacrosse brings you a lifetime of incredible memories. There's no doubt in my mind that the game will bring you numerous lifelong friendships, and experiences that you could have never had without being a part of the sport of lacrosse. So much of my life and the path that I have chosen have been directed by the game of lacrosse. I grew up playing in Sudlersville, Maryland for the Sudlersville Thunder, Lightning, and Storm teams, as well as the Eastern Shore All-Stars. I was a high school All-American at Kent County High School. I was a two-time All-American at Washington College, and coached at my alma mater for two years while getting my master's degree in History. I was drafted in 2005 to play professionally for the Los Angeles Riptide, and worked as a pro-sponsored athlete for Adrenaline Lacrosse in San Diego. Lacrosse has taken me across the country, and to places I could have never dreamed of going.

As I look back at having received the Turnbull Award my senior year at Washington College, I look back on that time in my life and think about how hard I worked to earn the Turnbull Award. I enjoyed my playing career immensely, and to be recognized as the top attackman in the country, and particularly in the name of a war hero is a tremendous honor. It is a reminder still today that hard work, and sacrifice pays off.

Some advice I might offer is to enjoy your time with each team you play on. The team always has to come first, and it's your job to put in the work to make sure you don't let your team down. Play other sports, so when you play lacrosse it is fresh and fun. Remember that is just a game and it's supposed to be fun. I think the lessons you will learn from your experience in lacrosse (and other sports) will prepare you for the challenges that you will encounter in adult life—so make the most of your learning opportunities.

I had some excellent coaches during my career, and they all constantly preached (and practiced) "Fundamentals, Fundamentals, Fundamentals." As a coach myself now for Shore Kaos Lacrosse, I have become more aware of the mental part of the game in addition to the physical part. Be a student of the game—there is so much to learn!

I hope the late Colonel Turnbull and his family would be proud of what I have tried to do to help my community through the sport of lacrosse. Perhaps they would be of you, as well!

My very best to you, Robbie.

Jon Fellows
Washington College 2002
Turnbull Award 2002

Dear Robbie,

My name is Gregory Cerar. I am a 2009 graduate of C.W. Post LIU where I received the Lt. Col. J. I. "Jack" Turnbull Award as the Outstanding Attackman in Division II in 2009 under head coach John Jez and his assistant Frank Vitolo. I grew up in Massapequa Park, New York, and was a graduate of Farmingdale High School. I was a multi-sport athlete who participated in golf, soccer, baseball, basketball and lacrosse. My father, being a baseball enthusiast his whole life, was taken aback when I decided to transition from baseball to lacrosse. I spent countless hours practicing with my lacrosse stick, perfecting my skills. My father would have his baseball mitt on always willing to have a catch with me as we learned the game together. Being small and extremely quick on my feet, I was able to excel in the sport of lacrosse at attack.

In my junior year of high school, I was contacted by many college lacrosse coaches. My dad and I were both excited about the possibility of a scholarship to help pay for college. We were amazed by the sheer number of letters and phone calls I received from collegiate coaches. I honestly found it extremely difficult to pick out that one school where I would commit so much of my time to a sport that I loved. I also wanted to pick a college where I would get a good education. It was a great honor to be considered by so many different colleges from all over the United States. During the fall of my senior year, I felt a ton of pressure with SAT's, ACT's and everyone wanting to know if and where I had decided to go to college. I visited many different schools, had several official visits and talked with many coaches. One of the last official visits was to C.W. Post located in Old Brookville, NY. After spending the weekend, and making some new friends, I finally made my decision to attend C.W. Post. I was also offered and an academic scholarship with my athletic scholarship, which helped me make my final decision. This choice would take me on a path that very few lacrosse players get to experience. Little did I know how important my decision would be.

As a college freshman, I practiced and played with six seniors who were starters on offense. I learned a lot that first year. I vividly remember the pressure to do well, to listen to the coaches, to have patience and, most of all, to be a team player. During my sophomore year, I was one of the few returning offensive players, which proved to be a rebuilding year. I was named captain in my junior year. I then assumed more of a leadership role. The team, once again, was unable to make it to the playoffs by one game. I took majority of the blame for the offense not showing up when the team needed us the most. I was forced to step it up and take charge of all six offensive players to get the best out of everyone on the field. I didn't want to go through another season with the feeling of letting the entire team down. In my senior year, I was able to figure out how to not only get the best out of my abilities, but to also get the best out of every player. We adopted the mentality that no defense could stop us if we all worked together as one. At the end of the season, we were able to accomplish our team goal by winning the National Championship 8–7 at Gillette Stadium. While the whole team was ecstatic that we won the final game, I was just relieved that I didn't let my team down. (I mean who wouldn't be, we now have a better winning percentage then Tom Brady does at home.) It was that year that I realized what the word "leader" meant to me. I believe there are many different ways of leading, but you cannot lead if you don't have anyone standing behind you who believe in you. Winning was great, but I wouldn't trade it for the friends I have made and the people who have supported me along my journey.

Being a Jack Turnbull Award winner is a great honor to me and my family. Being able to receive an award named after Lt. Col. J. I. "Jack" Turnbull, who did so much for not only the sport but for our country, is quite a privilege. I often think that my grandfather, who loved sports and served as a sergeant in the Korean War, would have been proud of me. Lacrosse has expanded exponentially in the last decade. It had a major impact on my life and taught me how to deal with any obstacle that comes my way. I hope that lacrosse will take you as far as it has taken me. If you keep working hard and remain positive–there is no telling what you can do.

Sincerely,

Gregory Cerar

C.W. Post-LIU 2009
Turnbull Award 2009

Dear Robbie,

Greetings. I am William C. "Bill" Stutt, Naval Academy, Class of 1949. I write to you on behalf of my late teammate, classmate, and roommate, J.H.L. "Lee" Chambers, who received the Turnbull Award way back in 1949.

Lee graduated from the McDonogh School in Baltimore and then from the Naval Academy. He had a fantastic lacrosse career at Navy. I think he is still their all-time leading goal scorer (they didn't keep assists back then). He was part of two National Championship teams (1946, 1949) and was a four-time All-American. He is a member of the National Lacrosse Hall of Fame (inducted 1975). He served in the U.S. Navy upon graduation and later in the Marine Corps before resigning to assume leadership of a family design business headquartered in Baltimore.

Lee was super modest. He acknowledged his awards but never really talked about them. He also received the U.S. Naval Academy Athletic Association Trophy for being the most outstanding athlete in his class.

Lee played crease attack. His size, strength, and hair-trigger reflexes enabled him to be a prolific scorer. He was not a dodger. The head of his stick was the size of a defensive stick (back then—much bigger than a normal attack stick), with little or no pocket. He would often receive a pass and shoot all in one motion without cradling. Because of his success and the close quarters with defensemen around the crease, Lee endured a lot of illicit contact, which the referees didn't see. But he never complained.

We played with a rectangular crease back then. I am not sure how playing with a circular crease would have affected Lee's play—just interesting to note, I think. Our offensive philosophy was "pass and cut," with minimal dodging. This style fit Lee perfectly.

I should also say that our sticks back then were very unique. Today they are much more uniform. We would spend hours at the Bacharach and Rasin store loft in Baltimore selecting three or four sticks that we thought had the best balance and feel.

Our coach, Dinty Moore (an all-time legend), had the annual challenge of developing part of his team from athletes who had never played before coming to the Naval Academy. Typically, they were defensemen of athletic talent who also played football. Those of us who had some stick skills from high school played midfield and attack. During our preseason, we had endless stick drills before starting scrimmages. Unlike the plebe coach (and later highly successful varsity coach, and another legend, Willis Bilderback), Dinty never had set "plays." The closest we got to "plays" were extra man drills. Interestingly, the Navy football coach, recognizing Lee's athletic abilities tried unsuccessfully to recruit him to play tight end in football, much to Dinty's chagrin, fearing his "Leecham" might get injured.

One of Lee's highlights would have been his play in the 1946 North-South All-Star game at Hopkins' Homewood Field in Baltimore when he scored seven goals in a 14-14 tie. Lee scored two goals in the last three minutes to tie the game and then scored again with 48 seconds to go in overtime after the North had gone up once more!

Our games with Army were always special. Both coaches, Dinty and Morris Touchstone at Army, always had Frenchy Julian as referee. I believe Frenchy was from Canada. He was fair and tolerated heavy contact.

Playing with Lee and the rest of my teammates at Navy was a very special time for me. We worked very hard but we also had a great time playing the game. A few of those friendships remain with me today—some sixty-five years later.

Lee played the game hard and fairly. He was a model of what we should all aspire to be as a player and teammate. It was a joy to play with him. In the really close games we could usually count on Lee for a goal or two that would make the difference … I suspect Lee would encourage you to perfect your talents through lots of practice.

On behalf of J.H.L. Chambers,

Bill Stutt

USNA 1949

Hi Robbie,

I am glad to hear of your connection to the history of the game of lacrosse. I am Joe High–Salisbury State University Class of 2000, where we won the national championship my junior year and I received the Turnbull Award as a senior.

Lacrosse has been a part of my entire life! I started playing at Cockeysville Rec in Maryland when I was five years old. I played at Dulaney High School and then went on to Salisbury. I still play today and love the game as much as I did as a kid under the lights at County Home Park. I got my first job through lacrosse, traveled the world through lacrosse, and even met my wife through lacrosse (she was an All-American at Salisbury, as well!).

Lacrosse is played by people with pride and dignity and that becomes more and more evident when you play at higher levels. It is similar to golf in that sense. There is a respect for the game and for others that play the game. That creates a community that takes care of each other through life.

I think if I could offer one piece of advice it would be to remember that you get out what you put in—whether in sports or your life in general. I think my coaches were always fair with me. I don't think you can ask for anything else. But as a player, I always felt it was my job to make myself better—not theirs.

Most people like to recommend books as a form of encouragement and spiritual drive. That isn't me. I recommend finding something you love doing and attack it at full speed. You don't need a book to tell you if you love the game of lacrosse. If you are exhausted at the end of a tough practice and look forward to getting after it the next day, you already know you love it; and putting the effort in will make you great at it. You can apply that to just about anything. Having said that, if you really love reading then I recommend *The Little Engine That Could*.

Keep working hard and enjoy the game. Make sure to thank all of the people who are making your lacrosse experience possible—the people who played before you, parents, coaches, officials, people who set up leagues, etc. You will never forget them.

As I said before, I owe nearly everything I have today to those people in my life: Coach Berkman and Hasbrouck (Salisbury), Coach Schreiber (Dulaney), Coach Davis and Miller (Cockeysville), Jason Coffman, Chris McQueeney, Erik Miller, Jayme Block, Jake Bergey, Jay Owen and the rest of the Seagull family that came before me and most importantly, my mom and dad. They all have something else they could be doing and very few of them are paid for the dedication they provide. Every one of them will make you a better player and a better person.

My very best, Robbie,

Joe High

Salisbury State University 1997–2000
Turnbull Award 2000

Dear Robbie,

Hi! I am Rob Pannell of the New York Lizards and I understand that you have the good fortune to be connected to some of the great players in history. Wow! I hope you get to enjoy it. Coach Scott asked me to share a few thoughts with you and I am very glad to do so.

My lacrosse experience has been all I could hope for and more. I have worked extremely hard and through a number of challenges (getting cut from my high school team as a freshman, breaking my foot at Cornell, not being "recruited" earlier in my career, among others) to get where I am today, but have been rewarded for it. Lacrosse has allowed me to give back to the sport I have come to love as well. I remember sitting in front of the TV as a child and watching players like Connor Gill of Virginia and admiring his playing style and wanting to be him, wanting to be playing on Final-Four weekend and my first year in college I found myself starting at attack in the National Championship game for Cornell. I remember these days so when given the chance to speak to a kid or make his day, I take it because I remember being in their position once. That is my favorite part of playing the game! It is very rewarding giving back to the sport which you have come to love and teaching those learning the game at a young age.

Receiving the Turnbull Award (twice) was an incredible honor, especially knowing the three people who received it prior to me at Cornell; Mike French, Eamon McEneaney, and Tim Goldstein. I have a tremendous amount of respect for these three individuals and aspire to be as good as them one day. I have had the privilege of meeting Mike and Tim but never Eamon (he passed away on September 11, 2001 in the World Trade Center), but being compared to him is the biggest compliment anyone could ever give me. I have heard he was an incredible lacrosse player but and even more incredible individual. To be a Turnbull award recipient–named for someone who is considered the greatest player ever and, more importantly, a man who gave his life for his country in World War II–and mentioned in the same sentence as some of the greatest players ever is truly an honor.

One piece of advice I would offer would be to never be satisfied with the player you are, for you will be passed by someone that is working harder than you each and every day. There is always something in your game that you can be working on no matter how good you think you are or whatever awards you have received. I still have that attitude today–even after winning two Jack Turnbull Awards, the Tewaaraton Award, playing professional lacrosse, and still being a member of the United States training team (I haven't made the final roster yet!).

I'd also say to do your best to live a well-balanced life that includes family first, religion, education, and lacrosse. The people in your family are those most important to you and those closest to you and you would not be where you are today without them. Lacrosse is important but your family relationships are more important along with religion. Receiving a great education is also important and getting the most out of the institution where you are receiving that education.

Our approach at Cornell was to outwork our opponents in every facet of the game which includes weight sessions, conditioning, practices, etc. and getting the very best out of every individual of the team to reach a common goal! Well done is better than well said!

Stepping out onto the field for the National Championship in 2009 was one of the more memorable moments of my career. Having dreamed about playing in the Final-Four my whole life, I couldn't believe it was actually happening and still haven't. It will finally hit me one day down the road what Cornell had accomplished in my time there!

It has also been an amazing experience being a part of the Cornell Lacrosse family in just the few years I have been a member myself. Every game, every event, every gathering among the Cornell Lacrosse Family is unlike anything I have seen with any other team. It is truly an amazing thing to be a part of, having alumni who care so much about their former team who they haven't played for in 5, 10, 20, 30 years, but still come back to support and celebrate their success. I wouldn't want to have played for any other school out there!

So many people have helped me in my career. I mentioned my family—but also Coaches Kevin Huff and Sean Keenan (Smithtown West) Chip Davis (Deerfield Academy) and Jeff Tambroni and Ben DeLuca (Cornell) as well as my all the teams I was a part of at Cornell were particularly supportive, helpful, and influential.

My book recommendation is *Training Camp: What the Best do Better than Everyone Else* by Jon Gordon!

I wish you all the best and hope that we will be able to meet in person at some point—I'd love to hear about your special stick.

Good Luck!

Go Big Red!

Rob Pannell

Turnbull Award 2010, 2011
Cornell University

Hi Robbie,

Hello from Upstate, New York–Homer to be exact. I am Matt Riter and am very glad to connect with you. I began playing lacrosse in a friend's backyard when I was in 5th grade. The minute I started playing, I was hooked! It has been a part of my life ever since. I played at Homer High School and then Syracuse University. I received the Turnbull Award after the 1993 season and was quite thrilled and honored. My teammate, Greg Burns, received it my freshman year and former Syracuse great John Zulberti had won it shortly before Greg. So I knew what a special award it was at the time. Looking back now, I think it means even more to me. I think I was lucky to be part of a team that made me look good. We had a bunch of excellent players but not the real "superstars" for which Syracuse had become known. We also won the national championship that year. That was pretty special, obviously, and also means more to me each year.

I have been coaching some very young players for the last few years and I'll share with you some things I usually say to them. First–keep your stick in your hands as much as possible. You have probably heard this a million times–but work on the wall. I used to use a basketball backboard since I didn't really have a good wall nearby out in the country. You can (and must) do all of this without other people. Use two hands. We start our little guys by simply flipping the ball up in the air to themselves. Be a smart player. Know what the play will look like a few steps ahead. Study the game. If you can't throw and catch then you can't play. You would be amazed at what second graders can do when they are coached well and practice. So get the work done so that you can get to your highest level.

I hope you realize, Robbie, what the game can do for you. You'll meet new people and you are very likely to make friendships playing the game that will last your whole life.

Among my most special memories in the game was a trip that our Syracuse team took to Lockerbie, Scotland in 1989 after a terrorist attack took down a plane carrying thirty-five of our students (and a total of 259 people on board and eleven people on the ground) back to Syracuse University after studying abroad. Coach Simmons thought it would helpful for our team to offer our support to the families–on both sides of the Atlantic Ocean–that suffered those terrible losses. It was my first time flying–so I was terrified. But we were welcomed with open arms by both England and Scotland. I remember that the fields were nice with short grass like putting greens, the weather in England was very gray and cloudy, and Scotland was beautiful with rolling, grassy hills with no trees. We did some clinics and exhibitions—it was the first time I had played international rules. We visited the memorial area, which was very symbolic of why we were there. I can still picture it in my mind today. It was an incredible trip.

Lacrosse has been very good to me. I hope you'll get to enjoy our great game as much as I have and that you'll be inclined, like so many of us who have had a great experience in the game, to give some of it back to younger players.

A book I would recommend you read is *The Boys of Winter: The Untold Story of a Coach, a Dream, and the 1980 U.S. Olympic Hockey Team* by Wayne Coffey because it shows that good coaching and hard work/perseverance pay off, and it stresses how rivals can come together and play as one to represent your country.

Good luck, Robbie,

Matt Riter

Syracuse University 1993
Turnbull Award 1993

Hi Robbie,

I am Bill Tanton writing to you on behalf of the late Emil A. "Buzzy" Budnitz Jr., in regard to the Turnbull Award he received in 1953. Coach Scott has briefed me on your relationship with Jack's family! Coach Scott, Buzzy, and I were teammates at Johns Hopkins.

Let me begin by saying that Buzzy Budnitz was a great lacrosse player. There's no doubt about that. That's why he's in the Lacrosse Hall of Fame. At the same time, he was one of the most unusual players I've ever seen in more than a half century in lacrosse. In fact, I can't think of a single player in any decade to compare with Buzzy–and I played with him on the Johns Hopkins teams in the early 1950's. What made him unique was that, while he was a great attackman all his career, at Baltimore City College, at Hopkins and then for a decade with the mighty Mt. Washington Club teams, he was deceiving. He was not big. He was basically slim, he was knock-kneed, and he was not fast afoot. But he was a masterful stick handler and when he had the ball in his stick–and he loved to carry the ball–something magic happened. He may have been the most accurate passer I've ever seen. I never saw him make a bad pass. And he obviously saw the field extraordinarily well.

I still remember one moment at practice, the team scrimmaging, Budnitz with ball behind the goal, me at crease attack, and Buzzy saw me open–he was uncanny at seeing things like that–and he fed the ball to me–a perfect pass into the sweet spot of my stick–and because I was slow at getting the shot off, a defenseman named Brooke Sheehan checked my stick, sending the ball to the ground. There was no goal–and this was just practice, remember–because I could not get the shot off. I remember this mere instant to this day because I remember saying to myself at the time, I'll never get a more perfect feed in my life than that one and I still couldn't do anything with it.

I know Buzzy as a competitor so well that I even played intramural basketball against him at Hopkins–and often guarded him in those games. Buzzy was an outstanding soccer player at Hopkins but in the winter he played basketball. I had been a high school basketball player. I don't think Budnitz played that sport at City and when we went head-to-head in the Homewood gym in December and January I thought I could eat him up. Hey, he was only this skinny, knock kneed guy who hadn't played basketball in high school. To my shock and annoyance, he got the better of me more often than the reverse. I guess you'd say he was sneaky quick as an athlete, because he excelled at taking the ball away from you. And when he drove to the basket he was past his opponent before the guy knew it. Basket by Budnitz.

I've often though Buzzy's lacrosse opponents may have underrated him because he didn't look like a great athlete. But he sure was one. A lot of actual great athletes were surprised when they paid a price when they made the mistake of underrating the attackman behind the goal at Hopkins and at the Mount in those days.

I hope you will enjoy playing the game as much–and as well and for as long–as Buzzy did and that you will be able to have a similar effect on it after it is all said and done. My very best wishes, Robbie.

Bill Tanton

JHU '53

[RHS Note: Bill has been a sports writer for over sixty years–about forty at the Baltimore *Evening Sun* and more recently as a columnist for *Lacrosse* Magazine, published by US Lacrosse.]

Dear Robbie,

I have been playing lacrosse as long as I can remember. I grew up in Baltimore, played at Loyola Blakefield High School, and just graduated from Dickinson College. Baltimore is a huge lacrosse town and growing up there really inspired my love for the game. To me, lacrosse is fun, plain and simple. I received the Turnbull Award last spring (2013) at Dickinson. I consider it a tremendous honor to be recognized in the name of one of the greatest players in the history of the game, and an admirable and intelligent leader. Since receiving the award, I have learned quite a bit more about Jack and he is now one of my role models because his talents and efforts went way beyond the sport of lacrosse, which is something I strive for, as well. Having a great team played a huge part of my recognition and my teammates made my job easy.

I would recommend that you work hard on your academics. I really cracked down the last couple of years and it has really helped me with my focus on and off the field. Coach Webster at Dickinson (and my high school coach, Jack Crawford) really emphasizes excellence in all areas–they genuinely want the best for each of us and that always starts with academics.

In terms of lacrosse, don't over-think the game. Just have a great time playing with all of your friends and you'll realize how fortunate we all are to compete together. I learned during an injury a few years ago how much I enjoyed the game. Watching while I healed was very difficult but also gave me a better appreciation for actually playing.

As you move along, you'll probably encounter a number of challenges. When things get tough, think 24 hours into the future and determine if persevering was worth it (it usually is).

I hope you enjoy learning more about the game, Robbie. It has been a true gift for me and so many others. I think if you treat the game well, it will treat you well in return. Keep working hard. I'd love to hear how things are going for you.

A book I would recommend to you is *Born to Run* by Christopher McDougall. The Superathletes in this book inspired me because they ran simply for enjoyment. I learned to embrace the struggle (of exercise, shooting, stickwork, schoolwork, etc.) and how rewarding it is to overcome it. I know that you would enjoy reading this book, as well.

All the best,

Brian Cannon

Turnbull Award 2013
Dickinson College 2014

Dear Robbie,

Thanks for letting me accompany you on your journey with your special stick. I am Mark Douglas, University of Maryland and Turnbull Award recipient in 1991. I grew up in Baltimore and learned to play lacrosse through though the local recreation league. After high school, I enlisted in the United States Marine Corps (I needed to do some growing up–so I thought that would be the best way) and served for four years. From there I went to the University of Maryland.

My father played professional hockey for the Toronto Maple Leafs. He was the first Defensive player ever to win Rookie of the Year in the NHL, and was on four Stanley Cup winning teams. He spent many years playing and coaching for the Baltimore Clippers, which is why I got introduced into lacrosse. I learned how to skate when I was 13 months old! As a kid, of course, I played hockey, but my mother pulled me off my hockey team because my grades weren't good enough. I hope you don't make the same mistake!

I attended a private boys' high school, Calvert Hall College High School, near Baltimore. My recreation coach Scott Calvert taught me to shoot to the open net and this was a great beginning. Scott became a great friend to me over the years, and still to this day. He also taught me to not be afraid to take chances, and reminded us that lacrosse was just a start point–that win or lose, enjoy everything about it and in your life.

After spending four years in the USMC, I was fortunate that Mike Thomas convinced Dick Edell to recruit me to the University of Maryland on lacrosse scholarship.

Receiving the Turnbull Award was a huge surprise. I remember that I almost fell off my chair when my name was announced at the banquet. To be in such great company is pretty overwhelming. I certainly would not have received the award without my teammates, parents, and coaches.

I could rattle off a long list of great memories of the game–which would include playing with and against the greatest players ever at Calvert Hall, Maryland, and for Team Canada, scoring five goals in a game against Johns Hopkins, and on and on. But what I take away from the game at this point is the fact that I was so fortunate to make the friendships that I did.

After I received the Turnbull Award I presented it to my rec coach Scott Calvert for all he had done for and meant to me! Don't ever forget the people who help you grow in life.

Dick Edell was my coach at Maryland. Anyone who has ever played for Coach Edell will tell you what a great experience it was and what an incredible mentor he is. He was a commanding presence (he's about 6'5"!) and we all considered him a second father. We never wanted to disappoint him. Dave Slafkosky, our assistant coach, was held in similarly high regard.

I would encourage you to remember that lacrosse is a team game. To do well in lacrosse (and just about anything), you need to learn to work with people and find ways to help other people succeed.

Robbie, I think what separates people is their love for the game. You can tell when people love what they are doing—it shows.

I try to give back to the game today by coaching some young players, and keeping in touch with my lacrosse team to support lacrosse events.

I would love to meet you in person, Robbie, so that I could share more of my passion for the game! Please let me know if I can help you.

If you get a chance and like to read, I would recommend *The Education of Little Tree* by Forrest Carter.

Good luck, Robbie,

Mark Douglas

University of Maryland 1991
Turnbull Award 1991

Hi Robbie,

I write to you on behalf of my late brother and teammate, Jeff Cook, Johns Hopkins '82. Jeff was a fantastic player—a three-time All-American, two-time Turnbull Award recipient (outstanding attackman), Enners Award recipient (player of the year), Team USA player (world champion), and is enshrined in the National Lacrosse Hall of Fame. I think his teammates (myself included!) considered him the epitome of what the game should be about—skilled, tough, hard-working, team-oriented.

Jeff began his career in the first grade at St. Paul's School and then went on to the McDonogh School in Baltimore and then to Hopkins. He benefited immensely from great coaching during his entire career. He had at least four or five Hall of Fame coaches along the way (as well a number of teammates now enshrined).

Receiving the Turnbull Award meant a great deal to Jeff. I think he would say that he was gratified (as with all of his many awards) to be recognized by the various coaches and committees. He knew that the hard work he put into playing the game he truly loved to the best of his ability was recognized and appreciated. He was shocked that he received the MVP in the '81 championship even though his team lost. He certainly would have traded that recognition for a win.

As a player Jeff would tell you to work hard and play to the best of your ability at all times. He would encourage you to go to the goal (can't score unless you do). And, mostly, no "dancing," as he used to say.

Jeff was remarkably humble. He always credited his teammates—even when he was clearly a central part of his team's success. He always told people he had great midfielders to play with. As all attackmen know—you can't score if you don't have the ball. So it was always nice to hear Jeff express that sentiment as a thank you to his teammates.

Jeff had osteomyelitis as a child and, after several surgeries, had to have hip replacement surgery at age forty. He battled through all of his injuries along the way in the same warrior-like fashion.

My mother would be happy if I told you a quick story about Jeff's rehabilitation from his hip surgery. When she took him to therapy one day—she noticed a (now famous) poster that STX Lacrosse had printed back in the '80s—of Jeff playing for Hopkins vs. North Carolina—hanging on the wall of the waiting room. She related to me, "When the nurse came back from taking Jeff to another room, I asked her if she knew who that was on the poster. Meanwhile, there were just two of us in the waiting room. The other person said, 'That's my son!' The person was the father of John Haus–the North Carolina defenseman playing against Jeff. I, of course, said, 'That's my son!' What a coincidence since neither of us knew one another." It is a small world, Robbie.

Jeff was one of the greatest to play the game, Robbie. I know that he would be thrilled to hear of your association with him through Jack Turnbull–another of the all-time greats. Keep working hard. Please let me know if I can share any more with you in regard to our great game or my brother.

Good luck, Robbie,

Craig Cook for
My brother and teammate Jeff Cook

Johns Hopkins University 1982
Turnbull Award 1981, 1982
Enners Award 1981
Team USA 1982
National Lacrosse Hall of Fame, Class of 2006

Dear Robbie,

It is a pleasure to connect with you in regard to the Turnbull Award which I received at the University of Maryland in 1954. I hope that you will get to enjoy the game as I much as I have as a player, coach (University of Maryland 1963–76), and spectator (my whole life!).

I was fortunate to get to play at Baltimore Polytechnic Institute "Poly," the Mount Washington Lacrosse Club, and the University of Maryland with many, many great players and several great coaches.

I also enjoyed immensely working with the young men at the University of Maryland during my coaching tenure there. I have been truly fortunate in the game.

I am particularly grateful to Gardner Malonee and Bill Logan who took me under their arms at a critical point in my development.

Perhaps I can pass along some lessons that were shared with me by many people:

• Get the loose ball.
• Go to the goal.
• Find the open man.

These three things haven't changed much since my days!

I would encourage you to always do the right thing and be honest.

My very best to you in your journey.

Rennie

C. Rennie Smith

Maryland '55

Hi Robbie,

I'm very pleased to connect with you in regard to my Turnbull Award in 2010 at Le Moyne College. I grew up in Syracuse New York, an area which is highly recognized for producing talented lacrosse players. I was very fortunate to have the opportunity to play against so many great players and teams. As a result of the level of competition surrounding me, it inspired me to become the player I became. I didn't start playing lacrosse until the 7th grade and it was solely because all of my friends played. I was immediately hooked and I fell in love with the game. I spent countless hours and days playing "wall ball" and shooting; every day trying to improve and enjoying every second of it.

Due in part to my commitment and love for the game but most importantly to what the award represented, it was a complete honor to have been awarded the Turnbull Award. I know that Jack was a tremendous player, athlete, and person, and that he died in the service of our country. I was so proud that I was awarded something that was representative of such a remarkable person.

Always remember that lacrosse is a team game, work hard, have fun and you will get out more from the game than you will ever imagine!

Best of luck,

Jack Harmatuk

Le Moyne College 2011
Turnbull Award 2010

Dear Robbie,

I was the Division II Turnbull Award recipient in 2000 and consider it one of my greatest athletic achievements. It brings me great joy to share my experience with the game of lacrosse with you in hopes that you can imagine the endless possibilities the game can bring to you in your life. I grew up in Holbrook, New York and started playing the game at a very young age. I was four years old when my parents enrolled my two brothers and me into the Sachem Athletic Club lacrosse program and we were all instantly hooked. After playing throughout my childhood and adolescent years, I was overjoyed that lacrosse was the reason I was offered a scholarship to play at CW Post, Long Island University.

The knowledge I have acquired from being on the field and part of a team has carried over into my adult life in the working world. You have to understand that my involvement with the game has been the gift that keeps on giving. I am so grateful. Lacrosse has given me the opportunity to play at the highest levels and travel world. As a youth player, we traveled the east coast of the US and Canada to play. My high school team played at the highest level and traveled to the New York State Division 1 championship, which unfortunately resulted in a loss. At CW Post, I was a four year starter, team captain; two time All-American Attackman in '98 and '00. My team and I played in three Division II National Championship games and lost all three years. I have learned that sometimes losing a game, especially one as important as state and national championship, is a greater lesson to learn than winning. It taught me humility and it fueled me to work harder. Losing is very powerful motivation. Regardless of the end result, every time I played with heart, I felt like a winner and felt good knowing I had given my all every time I walked off the field.

After college, I was accepted into English Lacrosse Program Delegation. The program's initiative was to teach the game to British youngsters. I was 21 years old, living in another country, coaching the sport I love. It was one of the best times of my life. I played for Team Wales in the 2002 World Lacrosse Championships in Perth, Australia. After the games, I went on to coach various varsity high school teams in New York and Ohio. I am 36 years old and am proud to say that I still play lacrosse to this day. I coach, along with my three brothers, for a well-respected travel organization that has teams ranging from 2nd grade to varsity level. I also am part of a training program, which provides players a unique method of learning specialty skills, taking them to the next level of playing.

In addition to coaching and training, I have been officiating games at the high school and college level for the past nine years. Officiating allows me to see the game from a different perspective and I learn something new with every game. If there is one thing I can do to give back to the sport, it is to share it with children so they can take away everything and more that I gained from it.

I have such respect for the sport after playing my entire life and watching it grow. It has given me opportunities that I could never have imagined in my wildest dreams. It is everything to me. It is and will always be my passion. I live, love, and breathe lacrosse. It has molded me into the man I am today. The determination, perseverance and discipline I've honed after the thirty-plus years of playing has greatly aided me in my career, where I feel I am able to exhibit leadership skills, commitment, and dedication to the team I manage.

I recommend that you take every valuable lesson you learn, cherish your teammates, as they will be your brothers on and off the field for the rest of your life, and hold on to every memory you make. Never give up, ever. The temptation to quit is usually the strongest when you are about to succeed. You are a competitor; use it to your advantage.

Receiving the Turnbull Award was a tremendous honor. I was being recognized for my achievements as a collegiate player and it validated all those years of hard work. Jack Turnbull was an amazing man and an inspiration to athletes in any sport.

A book that I would recommend you read is *The Art of War* by Sun Tzu. I find it fascinating that a guide to military tactics and strategy written thousands of years ago translates so well to life today. I leave you with a quote from it and hope you enjoy it as much as I have, "Victorious warriors win first and then go to war, while defeated warriors go to war first and then seek to win."

Best of Luck.

Gavin T. Chamberlain

CW Post Long Island University
Turnbull Award 2000

Dear Robbie,

I am thrilled to hear of your special stick and I am grateful for Coach Scott's invitation to connect with you. My name is Michael Watson and I received the Turnbull Award in 1996, while playing at the University of Virginia. I grew up playing in Baltimore, Maryland where I attended the St. Paul's School for Boys prior to matriculating at the University of Virginia.

My experience in the game has exceeded my wildest dreams. I have been fortunate at every stop on my journey–from youth league up through Team USA and Major League Lacrosse. I have learned from all of my teammates and coaches and consider myself extremely blessed to have had so many great people influencing me along the way.

Receiving individual honors such as the Turnbull Award gives you a sense of accomplishment–but I would be the first to tell you that my teammates and coaches all receive a piece of each of them.

I would encourage you to wake up each morning with a goal in mind to accomplish. Proceed on your journey with an open mind and a willingness to accept guidance from those who give it. For success is not merely an individual achievement, but a result of the influences that surround and shape you. I like baseball manager Sparky Anderson's quote, "Success isn't something that just happens. Success is learned, success is practiced, and then it is shared."

I thought you may enjoy reading a book by Malcolm Gladwell called *Outliers*. It raises some interesting questions that I think will help you along the way. Best of luck on your journey. Enjoy the ride…

All the best,

Michael Watson

University of Virginia 1996
Turnbull Award 1996
Team USA 1998
National Lacrosse Hall of Fame, Class of 2013

Dear Robbie,

I was a four year starting attackman at Washington College from 1980-1983. I was a two-time First-Team All-American, two-time team MVP, 1983 team captain, 1982 Division II/III HEROES award recipient, a member of Washington College's Hall of Fame, and I was the only Division III attackman to be named on the *Baltimore Sun's* All-America team in 1983. I also was a starting attackman on the South team in the annual North-South All Star game. In 1983, all divisions of lacrosse played in one game so it was a great honor to represent the South, with all of the other talented seniors. However, nothing means more to me than receiving the Jack Turnbull award in 1982.

The Lt. Col. J. I. Turnbull award puts a player in a unique category in lacrosse history. The award demonstrates absolute achievement through hard work, training, and determination.

Robbie, on January 3, 1981 I had major back surgery. I wasn't quite sure if I would be able to play lacrosse again, especially at a program like Washington College. But by our first game in March, I was back on the field as if nothing had happened. I really think the reason for my quick return was because I loved the game so much. Nothing was going to hold me back. As your lacrosse career moves forward, remember that adversity can never stop a motivated warrior. If you persist with great courage you can overcome any obstacle in life.

Lacrosse teaches one to be a better person. To be a great player, you must be unselfish, willing to overcome adversity at all costs, and be a leader. Lacrosse is a life lesson of teamwork and camaraderie. I carry this through life every day. I believe that if you follow your dreams, lacrosse will take you down that path for the rest of your life.

One of my favorite books to recommend to you is about the Lewis and Clark Expedition. It is titled *Undaunted Courage*, by Stephen E. Ambrose. The book exemplifies the will to succeed at all costs.

Regards,

Jeff Kauffman

Washington College 1983
Turnbull Award 1982

Dear Robbie,

What a pleasure to connect with you in regard to your special stick. Coach Scott has shared with me a little bit about your journey with Red Hawk and Captain Lewis. I am a bit jealous! I am John Kaestner from the University of Maryland. I received the Turnbull Award in 1972–so that is where you and I become connected. I played at a very interesting time in the game's history in that by my junior year in college the plastic stick was beginning to become common. Believe me, the new technology made a world of difference in my game. I had grown up with a wooden stick and not until my freshman year in college did I become proficient with both hands. The plastic stick was easy to "break in" and was balanced unlike the wooden ones. In fact the week before the Hopkins game my senior year I broke both my game sticks and that week I got two new sticks which I broke in in two days. On that Saturday at Hopkins on their homecoming against the number one team in the country, I had the day I had dreamed of as a ten year old fourth grader. The plastic stick enabled me to go from a two-time All-American to the Turnbull Award winner!

To say I grew up in a lacrosse family would be an understatement. My dad, Bud Kaestner, played at Johns Hopkins in the early forties and knew Jack Turnbull. He was selected to the national Hall of Fame as was my brother Hank, who also attended JHU, and was the first defender to receive the Schmeisser Award for the best defenseman in college twice! My other brother Reed was a two-time All-American and captain of my Maryland team in 1970. I have three children all of whom played Division I lacrosse. My oldest, Ashby, was a three-time All-American at Georgetown University and played on the US team for three years. My other daughter, Christie, started for four years at Duke University and was a First-Team All-American in her senior year. My son John played at JHU and had some great moments on the field and made friends for life with his teammates. All three love and honor the game all have been involved with passing on their skills and love of lacrosse to young players like you.

I started playing in the fourth grade at The Friends School in Baltimore and my dad showed me a diagram of a field before my first game on the Friends midget team comprised of fifth and sixth graders. He told me to call for the ball from my teammates and the go to the goal and score. I did that four times in that first game and boy was I hooked! I continued playing at Friends and made varsity my freshman year where the great Joe Cowan helped me get better. He was my hero then and this was before he was a Turnbull Award winner himself at JHU. I also remember watching my big brother, Hank, play against Captain Lewis, my other hero. My dad stood behind the goal and took home movies of two of the all-time greats in Jimmy and Hank! What a thrill to have heroes like Jim Lewis and Joe Cowan and to be mentioned in their company as a fellow Turnbull winner is truly a great honor and one I am humbled to have.

As I have said, my kids all played at the highest level of lacrosse and had great success. You can have a similar experience if you follow their plan. They realized that if they were great students, great players, and great people, they would have an opportunity to go to the college of their choice. To their credit, they all three achieved their goals, and you can too.

Dreams do come true with hard work and dedication.

Remember that the inscription on the Turnbull Memorial Trophy reads:

John G. Kaestner
Has been selected the outstanding collegiate attackman
during the 1972 Lacrosse season.
The recipient of this award best emulated the example of
Jack Turnbull in good sportsmanship, fair play, field leadership,
ability to both feed and score, and also to ride the defense.

As you can see, Jack Turnbull was most of all an honorable man, a good sport, a team leader, and a fine player. Robbie, I think you will find that those qualities will serve you well in life as they have for all the Turnbull winners and me. Do not be afraid to be great, be a good teammate, play hard, have fun, and let the special stick lead you to whatever you want to be.

I have been associated with lacrosse for 55 years, and one thing that I have found is that all lacrosse players have a special bond. My dad, Jack Turnbull, my brothers, my kids, and all who play today and came before us are at a certain level the same guy. We all honor those who came before and we all are obligated to pass down those values that we all share.

A book that you might like is *Wooden* by John Wooden and Steve Jamison—I think it is a good guide for life.

Robbie, all the best with your special stick and I look forward to watching you on the field someday.

Yours in sports,

John Kaestner

University of Maryland
Turnbull Award 1972

Robbie:

I am honored to write to you and urge you to continue to follow your passion through your special stick. No one ever knows when they are young boys what passions they will develop for whatever endeavor they take on as they grow up, but the sport of lacrosse seems to take hold of us and never lets go.

To me, Lacrosse has always been more than a sport. To many of us it becomes a way of life and the lessons we learn as players become those lessons that we pass on to the next generation as a coach and as a parent. Through lacrosse I have learned Life Lessons that I encourage you to remember and pass on to your friends and teammates and encourage these folks to do the same. Through Lacrosse, you will make friendships that will last a lifetime and develop a unique bond that just evolves from the sharing of a passion for our great sport. As a Coach, I carry with me the same level of passion that I had as a player. I love when I have discussions with young men that I coach and they say, "Coach, you really put a lot of hard work and effort in to being a success on the field." And my reply is always the same, "Funny, it has never felt like work to me." Once you cross the threshold into Passion, you will never think of anything you do with this great sport as Work.

I have learned from Lacrosse through the years the meaning of sportsmanship, camaraderie, integrity, and what it means to uphold these ideals in everything I do. Take the time to give back to others through your Love of the Game and teach others the same…it is magical.

Please consider reading *Success is a Choice* by Rick Pitino.

Continue your quest for Learning,

Paul Goldsmith

Roanoke College
Jack Turnbull Award, 1983

Dear Robbie,

Congratulations on being chosen to carry the stick. While preparing to write this letter I cannot describe the emotions it conjured up and the sense of gratitude I felt as I reflected on my lacrosse experiences.

Dave Urick, my coach at Hobart College, was a great teacher, mentor, and motivator. Coach Urick saw something in me when many others had doubts. He gave me a chance to play at Hobart, a school that had just won four consecutive Division III National Championships. And when the time was right, he had faith in me as a player—giving me the opportunity to succeed following in the footsteps of Hobart greats like Mark Darcangelo, Rick Gilbert, and Tom Grimaldi. I cannot thank Coach Urick enough for these gifts.

Robbie, Jack Turnbull Award winners are undoubtedly talented, but the people around them advance their achievements. As you get older and reflect back on what is sure to be a great career, you will think about the many amazing teams you played on, and how these teams helped contribute to your success. Attackmen have the good fortune to be the finishers of many great plays. But, at the start of many of these plays there will be a check, save, or groundball and the player that started the play will rarely get his name in the newspaper.

Peter Ortale (Penn Charter, Duke, NYAC) was one of those guys. He created opportunities for the attack to shine. Peter was my friend and teammate on the New York Athletic Club. He tragically lost his life in the World Trade Center on 9/11, but he truly represented so much of what Jack Turnbull was, in terms of physical and mental toughness. He was the consummate team player and always put others ahead of himself on and off the field. I wish my two sons could have known him.

Robbie, as you embark on this exciting journey I know you will be a part of many great teams. At the end of every great game and season think of the coach who had faith in you and your unsung teammates and remember to say "thank you."

Best wishes,

Ray Gilliam

Hobart College Division III National Champs 1984, 85, 86, 87
Turnbull Award 1986, 87
United States Club Lacrosse Player of the Year 1989
Hobart Athletic Hall of Fame 2000
National Lacrosse Hall of Fame, Long Island Metro Chapter 2001

Dear Robbie,

My daughters and I are so happy to be invited by Coach Scott to write to you. I am Peg Tunstall and my late husband, W. Brooke Tunstall, received the Turnbull award in 1947 and 1948 while playing for Johns Hopkins University. That was quite some time ago, but all of our memories of Brooke are vivid and filled with joy and pride.

I must begin by telling you that next to Jack Turnbull, Brooke loved and respected no person more than Coach Scott, who was kind enough to come to Brooke's gravesite and offer his eulogy, a tribute that would have made Brooke smile with happiness and pride. After Coach Scott's remarks, two Marines folded the American flag that had been draped over his casket, and presented it to my daughters and me. To have Brooke's life end with Bob Scott's remarks and Marines presenting our family that flag summarized the cherished values that inspired Brooke's life and will follow him forever. We will never forget Bob Scott's kindness to us all these years and in that particular case.

Brooke was a wonderful, wonderful husband, father and grandfather, as well as an extraordinary athlete, successful corporate executive and respected writer.

He excelled in many sports, but his passion was Lacrosse and, though he didn't talk much about it, from what we heard and read, Brooke was one of the all-time great players in lacrosse history. And we think that if he were here, he would tell you that what he cherished the most in his experience was the influence that older players had on his development as a player and as a person.

Brooke had the great good fortune to grow up in a small suburb of Baltimore (Mount Washington), where the Turnbull family lived. Mount Washington had a club Lacrosse team and their field was just a quick bicycle ride from Brooke's house. It was there Brooke headed every day after school and watched Jack Turnbull and some top lacrosse being played and coached by top coach "Kid" Norris. Brooke became water boy and ball boy for the Mt. Washington teams on which Jack played in the 1930's. Jack became Brooke's role model.

The classic, impressive playing skills, and the character values and standards of conduct that he observed in the Mount Washington players and teams became a part of Brooke throughout his life.

I think if Brooke had been alive to receive this request from Coach Scott, he very likely would have sent you, in addition to a nice letter, something by which to remember Jack. He did things like that all the time! So we send to you a cherished penny that Jack gave Brooke around 1937 or so. Jack apparently had found it on the field at the Olympic Games in Los Angeles, and carried with him for years for good luck. He passed it along to Brooke, who did the same. We are certain that he would want you to have this penny and to keep it as a reminder of Jack. We hope it brings you the same amount of luck it did to Jack and Brooke!

I thing Brooke, who was an eternal optimist, would tell you, Robbie, to take the game seriously, but not so much yourself. It is a TEAM GAME and it is fun to play!

Brooke loved all history books and the *Great Books* series. He especially liked Ralph Waldo Emerson *Essays*, especially the one on "Self Reliance."

Brooke wrote an editorial piece for US Lacrosse magazine a few years ago sharing his experience in the game and a vision for its future. My daughter Tricia has edited it down to Brooke's "Code of Conduct" recommendation for you. Please see the enclosed copy. We hope that you will be able to extract just a few items to incorporate into your thinking.

We wish you all the very best, Robbie,

Peg Tunstall,

Paige Tunstall Gilberti, Tricia Tunstall, Leslie Tunstall
for W. Brooke Tunstall
Turnbull Award 1947, 1948
Turnbull-Reynolds Trophy 1947, 1948
National Lacrosse Hall of Fame, Class of 1977

LACROSSE PLAYERS' CODE OF CONDUCT

This Code is based on the premise that:

The long, rich history of sportsmanship and fair play unique to the game of lacrosse throughout its history and the love and commitment both current and past players have felt for the game deserve to be nurtured and preserved.

It is hoped that this Code, represented as a list of shared values, can be useful to lacrosse programs including grade schools, high and private prep schools, colleges, professional leagues, club teams and by players themselves as guidelines for lacrosse players on and off the field.

#1 BE TRUSTWORTHY
Act at all times with integrity, honesty, loyalty and commitment.

#2 HONOR THE GAME OF LACROSSE
Know and honor its history, its uniqueness and its rules—both in letter and in spirit.

#3 RESPECT LACROSSE AUTHORITIES
Behave respectfully towards coaches, referees, school administrators and staffs.

#4 PRACTICE UNSELFISHNESS
Place the interest of the team above one's own personal interest.

#5 BE A WORTHY ROLE MODEL FOR YOUNGER PLAYERS
Set an example for younger players to imitate and emulate.

#6 STRIVE TO IMPROVE YOUR SKILLS AND KNOWLEDGE OF THE GAME
Cultivate self-discipline in pursuing mastery of the skills and knowledge demanded by the game.

#7 CONTROL YOUR LANGUAGE AND BEHAVOIR ON AND OFF THE FIELD

Remember that profanity, obscene gestures and demeaning behavior diminish not only the player's own image but the team's character and the reputation of the game of lacrosse.

#8 MAKE YOUR ACADEMIC PURSUITS YOUR HIGHEST PRIORITY

Consider yourself a student-athlete—in that order. It is a priority that will serve you well for many years after college.

#9 OBSERVE STRICT TRAINING RULES

Lacrosse offers a unique opportunity to enjoy the experience of being in top physical condition. Combined with a balanced diet, good sleep regimens, the strict avoidance of alcohol or substance abuse, this results in top performance on the field.

#10 BE A GOOD CITIZEN IN THE SURROUNDING COMMUNITY

Support of and participation in local community redounds to the advantage of the team's reputation and the community's support of the lacrosse program.

Dear Robbie,

I hear you are the owner of a very special lacrosse stick. Learning the story of your stick reminds me of how I started playing lacrosse myself. A hockey teammate, named Drew Bucktooth, invited me to try out for the lacrosse team on his Indian reservation. Drew lived on the Onondaga reservation in Syracuse. The Onondaga people are a part of the Iroquois Nation. His family had been playing lacrosse for a long time. His father, Freeman "Boss" Bucktooth, was the team's coach and he had played at Syracuse University. On that team we played box lacrosse, which was 5 on 5 and played within a hockey rink (no ice of course) with a much smaller net. Needless to say, it was great to learn the sport amongst those whose forefathers invented it.

Lacrosse brought me to a lot of places both literally and figuratively. With the Onondaga team, I would spend the summers traveling all over Canada to play in various tournaments. Thanks to the skills I developed on the reservation, I had the opportunity to attend a boarding school in New Hampshire, Phillips Exeter Academy. New Hampshire was a place I had never been, but more importantly, at Exeter I received an unparalleled education. On the lacrosse field, I was proud to be a member of a team that went from having three wins my first season to 15 my senior year. Thanks to my success on the Exeter lacrosse team, I then went on to play for Middlebury College. Not only was Middlebury a great academic institution, but its lacrosse team had just won its first National Championship before I arrived and would go on to win two more during my tenure.

Most importantly, lacrosse introduced me to many influential people. Looking back on my lacrosse career the thing that I value the most are the relationships that I formed with my teammates and my coaches and the lessons they taught me.

Analogies between sports and life are made so frequently they can sound cliché. But clichés are often true. My college coach, Erin Quinn, used to often say that the success of the season wasn't defined by the final score, it was the locker room, the stretching, the practices, the bus rides and the way we played: The Journey. I believe that holds true in life Robbie. Enjoy the ride.

Michael Saraceni

Turnbull Award Recipient
Middlebury College '04

Dear Robbie,

I write to you on behalf of my late teammate, Oliver "Corky" Shepard, who received the Turnbull Award in 1950 at Johns Hopkins University. Corky and I were senior co-captains in 1950, and we had the honor of placing the flags on the nets of the goals, a ceremony, I understand, with which you are familiar.

Corky was a very important player for our Hopkins team. Our coach, Howdy Myers, had always considered Billy Hooper the outstanding assist man on his St. Paul's teams (Billy left to go to UVA) and it meant so much to our Hopkins team that Corky grew into that role of being an outstanding feeder. He was a key to our many victories. Corky brought a contagious enthusiasm and very positive attitude to our team. He always did his best and set high standards for all of us. Corky and I were teammates at Mt. Washington after graduating from Hopkins, playing for our great coach, Kid Norris. It was certainly an honor for me to play with him and remains friends for sixty-some years!

In regard to your special stick and Jack and Doug Turnbull, I grew up in Mt. Washington (as did Corky–but he played at Poly, where Jack and Doug played), close to where they grew up. I never knew Jack Turnbull, but knew Doug and various other members of the family. The entire Turnbull family were inspiring and generous people and excellent examples by how they lived, providing lessons for all of us in how to live. They were respected and admired by everyone in our community.

Robbie, all of us who attended St. Paul's school back then experienced the spirit of our great game as it lurked in every room and hallway. We carried our stick with us wherever we went–even to bed. When we went to class, we lined our sticks up on the wall outside of the classroom. Coach Myers was the stimulus for this, and the entire faculty backed it up. I think it instilled a sense of pride in us and, much more importantly, served as a tangible and visible reminder that being able to play lacrosse every day was a privilege–not a right–and that we had better get the job done in school in order to get to play that day!

I understand that you are also connected to Captain Jim Lewis through your stick–wow! I was the head coach at West Point for twelve years including the time when Jim was at Navy. The Army-Navy games were always memorable. Jimmy Lewis was the best player we ever came up against anywhere. Even after our "civil wars," their coach, Willis "Bildy"

Bilderback and I were good friends and always got together in the summer at Ocean City, Maryland, and often went fishing together.

I am so glad to have connected with you on behalf of Corky–we were truly fortunate to play at Hopkins with so many great players–one of whom, Wilson Fewster, passed away just recently.

I recently read a book about the Navy SEALS that I would recommend– it's called *Lone Survivor* by Marcus Luttrell with Patrick Robinson…an eyewitness account of Operation Red Wings. I hope you enjoy reading it as much as I did.

All the best, young man. If you are a fraction as fortunate in the game of lacrosse as Corky and I were–you are in for quite a treat!

Jim Adams

Johns Hopkins University 1950

[RHS Note: Robbie, Jim was one of my teammates at Hopkins! The US Lacrosse Men's Collegiate Officials Committee presents the James "Ace" Adams Sportsmanship Award to deserving teams every season. From a press release: "Initiated in 2006, the awards are presented annually to the college or university in each of the 11 officiating districts whose coaches, players, and fans exhibit the best sportsmanship throughout the season. The award exemplifies the tradition of sportsmanship in lacrosse displayed by Ace Adams, who amassed 284 collegiate victories during a coaching career that spanned across five decades and included stints at the United States Military Academy (Army), University of Pennsylvania, and University of Virginia. At the time of his retirement in 1992, Adams had the most wins of any active NCAA Division I coach. He was inducted into the National Lacrosse Hall of Fame in 1975."]

Dear Robbie,

I hope you are enjoying the start of summer and taking your special stick everywhere you go, even if it's a baseball game! I am humbled to share my story with you about my experience playing lacrosse and grateful to Coach Scott for the privilege to share it with you.

In the spring of 1979, I stood patiently waiting for my friends to come out of our middle school locker room to start our baseball practice, that's right, baseball! To my surprise they walked out carrying lacrosse sticks and looked at me confused. I quickly got on board, ran back into the locker room, crossed my name off the baseball roster and ran over to the lacrosse field to begin my journey in 7th grade.

My journey in this sport has been truly humbling and medicinal in miraculous ways. I have been blessed with championships at the high school, college, and coaching level, while also honored with humbling awards that are dedicated in memory of great people and lacrosse players such as Jack Turnbull.

However Robbie, I have come to understand how truly special this great sport was to my survival when I received news on Sunday October 1, 2000, that my health had failed. Unfortunately, my young friend, my body had a 15 centimeter mass growing in my chest cavity that did not belong there. I was dying.

My road to recovery started immediately at Johns Hopkins Weinberg Center in Baltimore, Maryland. To make a long story short, I battled for eight tough years to get my body back to good health, I survived.

However, over those eight years, I had come to understand that lacrosse was not just a game to me, it was survival. I had played this great game with passion, but all along I was being led by great leaders, coaches and teammates, who were teaching me life lessons in discipline, respect, perseverance and, most of all, faith in God. I was blessed with unbelievable support from family, friends, former teammates, and the lacrosse community altogether at the youth, high school, college, and professional level. Their love and support gave me great strength to physically and mentally battle my disease and survive.

In closing my note to you Robbie, I would like to share some special advice with you. Success in life is not granted, it's earned by those who are not afraid to fail and are willing to find the answers to succeed no matter how many times they fail.

Trust all who love you and put your faith in God, because with God in your life anything is possible.

Sincerely,

Tom Gravante

Men's Lacrosse Coach, Mount St. Mary's University
Hobart College 1988
1988 Turnbull Award Recipient

Dear Robbie,

So I understand you found the great game of lacrosse. You may want to double-knot your shoelaces because this is going to be the ride of your life.

My name is Darren McGurn, and I grew up in Chester, New Jersey. I was lucky enough to be introduced to the game of lacrosse at the age of 5 (1979). I am the youngest of four boys and my oldest brother, Mike, made the great leap from baseball to lacrosse his sophomore year in high school. With Mike's fascination of the physicality, speed, and grace of lacrosse, all three of his younger brothers craved the chance to play. At this time, our town didn't have a youth lacrosse program. My father, Ron McGurn, decided to start the Chester Lacrosse program with the help of the Police Athletic Association. This program is still running today and has produced thousands of lacrosse addicts like you and I.

For me, lacrosse has always been about my family and friends. All four of my brothers played college lacrosse, Mike McGurn (Brown University), Bryan McGurn (University of Hartford), Kevin McGurn (Ohio Wesleyan University). I played at Ohio Wesleyan and was a four-time All-America selection. I won the Turnbull Award in 1998 as well as being named the Iroquois National Player of the Year. I was also fortunate enough to be inducted into the New Jersey Lacrosse Hall of Fame (2003) and Ohio Wesleyan Hall of Fame (2009). My brothers played such a key role in my success and what truly made lacrosse fun. We spent countless hours in our backyard shooting on our goal and making up games to challenge each other for bragging rights at the dinner table. Today, I know that each day we played, I was refining my game; at the time, we were just having fun. There is no replacement for putting time and effort in to the game.

Receiving the Turnbull Award was an amazing cap to my college career. I owe so much of my success to my teammates, coaches, and family who pushed me to achieve such great heights. So many of my teammates are lifelong friends. My coaches are not only great coaches but also great friends. Lelan Rogers and John Zulberti (Turnbull Award Recipient '88 and '89) played a key role in my success. My brothers Mike and Bryan both coached me in high school. Mike was my head coach at Mendham High School and Bryan was an assistant coach my senior year. Mike Fuller coached me at Bridgton Academy in 1994. Coach Fuller was a great mentor, a great coach, and a great friend. Coach Fuller guided me through my recruiting process and introduced me to coaching summer lacrosse camps in Wilton, Connecticut. My college success would never have happened without Coach Fuller's mentoring. I was fortunate to have learned from some of the best coaches, but the lesson here is to listen to your coaches and learn from your teammates. Every practice and every game is an opportunity to improve.

If I can give you any words of wisdom, Robbie, it would be to treasure the game of lacrosse and the people you will meet along the way. Lacrosse will introduce you to amazing people who will impact you for a lifetime. The lessons learned with go well beyond the lacrosse field. These lessons will shape who you become. Now, as a part-time high school lacrosse coach in Atlanta, I see the importance of the little things in the game. I'm proud to see these guys graduate and go on to play in college and beyond.

Best of luck Robbie and enjoy the ride.

Cheers,

Darren McGurn

Ohio Wesleyan University
Turnbull Award 1998

Dear Robbie,

I cannot express enough how excited I was meet you and Captain Lewis—that is some "magic" lacrosse stick you have, full of so much history!

Lacrosse has played such an enormous role in my life since I received my first wooden stick when I was 12.

I learned that lacrosse had two major components in my life, both being spiritual in nature. The first was the lesson of hard work that my first stick taught me. I had to use the wall at my school to learn to catch, throw, pick up ground balls and develop little tricks that later made my career so much more enjoyable. I used that wall to develop all the basic skills that served my own career so well. Having a speech impediment for many of my early years, I found that stick was my way of speaking without having to say a word.

The second lesson I learned was that great people would enter my life to guide me on the right trail for a healthy, wholesome, spiritual life. From Bill Wormuth, my West Genesee High School Varsity lacrosse coach, to Lloyd Elm, Junior Varsity coach at West Genesee, originally a Lafayette High School graduate. He eventually returned to the Onondaga Indian Reservation School to lead that program and their young warriors to many championships and life-changing programs to better the fate of the Onondaga Nation in Syracuse, New York.

Probably the most influential coach in my career was the great Johns Hopkins All-American attackman, Jerry Schmidt (Turnbull Award 1962). He was my coach and mentor at Hobart College and gave me the space to become the attackman I grew into. My heart will always go out to him and his silent but strong direction in my life on and off the field.

One more thing Robbie, I would like to recommend a book for you to learn the spiritual basis of the life that we so much cherish in this wonderful country. It is *America's Prophet* by Bruce Feiler. This book will hopefully help explain the basis of the rules that guide us and where they originated.

To conclude Robbie, the stick and its contents, and the men that possessed it before you, were all great men that gave so much to their country, their families and the game they respected so much. I do hope you learn from it and soak in all the positive energy that it possesses and enjoy the trail it leads you to follow in the footsteps of Lt. Col. John I. "Jack" Turnbull. Congratulations!

Rick Gilbert

Hobart College, Class of 1974
Turnbull Award, 1974
Hobart College Hall of Fame Inductee, 1989
Inductee of the Greater Baltimore Chapter,
of the US Lacrosse Hall of Fame, 1999

Dear Robbie,

Congratulations on earning the special stick and thank you for picking up this letter. I hope you enjoy reading it as much as I enjoyed putting pen to paper.

I love the sport of lacrosse for the same reasons most people do. It's beautiful to watch, combining great individual creativity with graceful teamwork. It has hard-hitting and ballet-like finesse. It has great people playing, coaching and supporting it. If you make it a meaningful part of your life, it can create a network of friends and business relationships that will be with you forever. But above all, I loved lacrosse because it was my way of showing my parents how much I loved them.

I am the middle child of five in a middle class family. The tuition at Hopkins in 1992 was far more than what my family could afford. When I found out I got accepted but wouldn't receive a scholarship I was disappointed but understood that I couldn't attend. I remember thinking, the other more-affordable schools are not Hopkins, but they would be fine and I'd make the best of it. I'll never forget when my father came to me and said, "You are going to Hopkins. We will make it work for one year but you have to go and blow them all away and earn a scholarship for the next three years." My freshman year I tied the freshman record for goals and points earning All-American honors and a full athletic scholarship. I graduated the leading scorer and point producer in the school's storied history. I won the Enners Award and Turnbull Award for Best Player and Best Attacker, respectively.

I'm grateful for all of my teammates and coaches over the years. I played with (and for) some of the greats. Many of my goals were the result of a great play made by Brian Piccola or Dave Marr during my playing days at Hopkins, but I never would have been there had it not been for my Parents' great sacrifice. I loved to play for them.

I was told long ago when I first started playing, "If you love lacrosse, it will love you back ten times as much." I hope you love it, Robbie and I hope you can find a special fulfillment in it like I did.

Thank you for reading my letter. I wish you a great lacrosse journey.

Warmest regards,

Terry Riordan

Johns Hopkins 1995
Turnbull Award 1995

Hi Robbie,

My good friend and teammate Michael French has informed me that Coach Scott has invited all Turnbull Award recipients to write a short note to you in relation to your magic stick. Mike has asked me to write to you on behalf of our late teammate, Eamon McEneaney Cornell '77. What an honor to be asked to do so. I should begin, I think, by telling you a bit about Eamon and his career.

Eamon played at Sewanhaka High School in Floral Park, Long Island for the legendary coach Bill Ritch. Eamon then attended Cornell University and played for three years on the varsity (back then freshman were ineligible for varsity competition). He was a First-Team All-American and First-Team All-Ivy for his three varsity years. He won three Ivy League championships, two national championships, and was the MVP of the 1977 National Championship game. He received the Jack Turnbull Award as the Division I Attackman of the Year, the Lt. Raymond Enners Memorial Award as the Division I Player of the Year, played in the 1977 North-South Collegiate All-Star game, was enshrined in the National Lacrosse Hall of Fame in 1992, and received the *Tewaaraton Legends* Award in 2012. He also played football at Cornell. I could go on and on about a lot more accomplishments.

Eamon had two distinct parts to him; his athletic attributes and his keen intellect. He pursed both with full focus, commitment, and joy. While most people saw his athletic side in action, he never sought the limelight (that said, he was hard to miss with his long, flowing blonde hair, skinny legs, and his fiery demeanor). He cherished his time at Cornell, and his ability to be part of the literary scene there. He was always seeking wisdom and enlightenment.

Eamon was a truly fantastic player—one of the greatest ever to play. To get to play with him at Cornell was an experience none of us will forget. His passion and spirit for the game were unmatched. Cornell University and the entire game of lacrosse remember Eamon fondly. I have been fortunate to stay connected to Cornell and many of my teammates and coaches all these years (my son played there, too!).

One unique feature that Eamon brought to the table, which is truly a gift, was his ability to make those around him better. His work ethic and ability to believe deeply in himself, was evident to all who were around him. The great UCLA basketball coach, John Wooden (of whom we were great admirers), commented that, "A player who makes a team great, is more valuable than a great player." Eamon was that kind of player.

What is far more important than all of the well-deserved accolades that Eamon accumulated, is the person and player he was. I can tell you from a teammate's perspective that Eamon represented everything that is good about the game and in athletics. He was totally dedicated to his game–he did the work necessary to be great–and his teams, but he was also a scholar, a poet, and a great husband and father and friend to all.

Eamon passed away in the attacks of September 11, 2001 at the World Trade Center in New York. Eamon was also in the World Trade Center in 1993 when a terrorist attack took place and he was the first to help people during that incident and likely saved dozens of lives with his courage, selflessness, and leadership.

The Cornell University Press published Eamon's poems under the title *A Bend in the Road*. Eamon's wife, Bonnie, is also a published author, writing *Messages: Signs, Visits, and Premonitions from Loved Ones Lost on 9/11*. I would commend either one or both of those books to you.

We should all be so lucky to have played with people like Eamon. He truly is one of the most–if not *the* most–amazing people I have known in my life. He played–and lived his life–with a genuine fire. There were never enough hours in the day for Eamon to impact people, work on all of the things he wanted to do, to help make things better for people, not to mention being the husband and father that he was. The world lost a true hero and incredible person on 9/11 (as well as the other 3,000 people).

Coach Scott invited us to offer some advice about the game and life in general. I think Eamon's advice to you in regard to lacrosse would be to strive to be your very best, to enjoy every second of the experience, to find ways to make your teammates better, and to represent the game in a positive manner at all times.

I think the life advice Eamon would probably offer would be very similar–work hard, enjoy the journey, help people. But Eamon never "lectured" people to tell others how to live their lives. He believed all people should follow their hopes and dreams, and "be the best they can be," wherever their life journey took them. He did however have some thoughts on what helped him in his journey. We call them:

"Eamon's Points of Life"
1 - Love is Light
2 - Family and Friends

3 - Honesty, Humility, and Curiosity
4 - Spirituality
5 - Poetry, Literature, and Music
6 - Laughter and Wit
7 - Hard Work, Toughness, and Tenacity
8 - Athletics and Physical Fitness
9 - Passion, Purpose, and Heart
10 - Leadership
11 - Kindness

I would hope that you could use the example the Eamon left to all of us, Robbie. Be good, strong, and courageous, and look for ways to make the world a better place. Eamon certainly did. Mike and I–along with all of Eamon's teammates–wish you nothing but the best.

Eamon was truly a remarkable person and a "true brother." We miss him dearly.

All The Best,

John "Jake" O'Neill for my teammate

Eamon McEneaney
Cornell University 1977
Turnbull Award 1975
Enners Award 1977
Team USA 1978
Tewaaraton Legends Award 2012

Robbie,

I hope you realize how much I have enjoyed getting to know you and accompanying you on your journey over these last several months. Thank you for attending the Tewaaraton ceremony–it was a wonderful evening for me. It brought back so many great memories of my playing days and it was an honor to be there with those great college players.

The physical award is a 12-inch figure mounted on hexagon-black granite and polished wood. The hexagonal base symbolizes the six nations of the Iroquois Confederacy: the Mohawk, Cayuga, Oneida, Onondaga, Seneca, and Tuscarora tribes. They say the stick is a replica of a pre-1845 Cayuga stick. To me, Robbie, the Lacrosse stick being held represents one that you have become very familiar with.

I told a reporter that a reason that our championship teams were so successful was that we were at peace with whom we were and in love with the game and how we played. That was many years ago. What I didn't say should be very obvious. I was there that evening, receiving the award because of the great game of Lacrosse. What success I enjoyed in Lacrosse and in life was built upon core values....values that helped me on that journey; love, honesty, respect, discipline, determination and generosity. The six sides of the foundation of the trophy may also represent these six values. By now you should realize that these values are not only the keys to success on the Lacrosse field. They are just as important to the challenges of daily life. I think that might sum it all up.

Good luck to you as you continue your journey. Please let me know if there is anything I can do to help you.

Sincerely,

Jim

Jim Lewis
United States Naval Academy, Class of 1966
Turnbull Award 1964, 1965, 1966
National Lacrosse Hall of Fame 1981
Tewaaraton Legends Award 2014